# How to Bond With an Aquarius

Real Life Guidance on How to Get Along
and Be Friends with the
Penultimate Sign of the Zodiac

# How to Bond
# With an
# Aquarius

Real Life Guidance on How to Get Along
and Be Friends with the
Penultimate Sign of the Zodiac

## Mary L. English

BOOKS

Winchester, UK
Washington, USA

First published by O-Books, 2011
O Books is an imprint of John Hunt Publishing Ltd., The Bothy, Deershot Lodge, Park Lane, Ropley,
Hants, SO24 0BE, UK
office1@o-books.net
www.o-books.com

For distributor details and how to order please visit the 'Ordering' section on our website.

ISBN: 978 1 84694 433 8

A CIP catalogue record for this book is available from the British Library.

Design: Stuart Davies

Printed in the UK by CPI Antony Rowe, Chippenham, Wiltshire
Printed in the USA by Offset Paperback Mfrs, Inc

We operate a distinctive and ethical publishing philosophy in all
areas of its business, from its global network of authors to
production and worldwide distribution.

# CONTENTS

*I enjoyed this book very much. With the help of some spot-on quotes and insights, Mary English's guide to Aquarius takes you on a journey from the inner-space to the outer-reaches of the true maverick of the zodiac. You'll have fun exploring the paradoxes of the weird and wonderful Water Carrier, and learn much from this independent-minded sign – one that insists on taking the road less travelled.*
**Frank Clifford**, Astrologer and Principal of the London School of Astrology, www.londonschoolofastrology.co.uk

*Astrology can be a complicated craft but Mary makes it accessible and fun. This book is full of useful insights. Her writing style is fluid and charming. (Aquarian with Moon in Sagittarius and Libra rising)*
**Lucy English**, Senior Lecturer in Creative Writing, Author of *Selfish People*, Novelist and Poet

*Full of hints and tips, wisdoms and insights - "How to Bond with an Aquarius" is an invaluable aid to understanding and appreciating the Aquarian in your life.*
**Sally Morningstar** Dip.V.Med -, Author of *The Art of Wiccan Healing* and a Life & Soul Coach

*What I love about Mary's book is the unique approach she takes to help us understand and relate better to each of the 12 signs - in this case, Aquarius. Taking the main stumbling blocks of the average Aquarian we are suitably guided to a place of understanding and solution. If only we were given such a user manual for each sign early in life, we might all be more accepting of each other's differences and the world might be a nicer place.*
**Donna Taylor**, Author of *How to use the Healing Power of Your Planets.*

Also by Mary L English

6 Easy Steps in Astrology
How to Survive a Pisces (O-Books)
The Birth Charts of Indigo Children

Please visit Mary's site at www.maryenglish.com

Dedication

This book is dedicated to my Auntie
Barbara Heloise Elizabeth Gibbings
27 Jan 1917- 11-Dec 2008

A true Aquarius

# Acknowledgements

I would like to thank the following people:

My Aquarius mother Jean English, who was excited that I was writing another book.
My Aquarius sisters Lucy and Emily for being part of my family
My Aquarius ex-mother-in-law Maggie for being so friendly
My son for being the Libran that makes me always look on the other side.
My Taurus husband Jonathan for being the most wonderful man in the world.
Mabel, Jessica and Usha for their Homeopathic help and understanding.
Laura and Mandy for their friendship.
Donna Cunningham for her help and advice.
Frank Clifford and Donna Taylor for their time and encouragement
Alois Treindl for founding the wonderful Astro.com website.
All at the Bach Centre for keeping the Essences Alive
John my publisher for being the person that had faith in me and all the staff at O-Books
including Stuart, Trevor, Kate, Catherine, Maria, Mary and Carolyn who kindly edited it. Marina, Fynn Willis and Patricia Jeffery for their welcome editing eyes.
And last but not least my lovely clients for their valued contributions.

# Introduction

*"... there is no gate, no lock, no bolt that you can set upon the
freedom of my mind."*
Virginia Woolf 1.

Astrology has taken many forms over the years. From its beginnings in Babylon to its heyday in the medieval ages, it's still with
us and it still influences our thoughts and decisions.

Originally it was used to make sense of the weather and help
with crop planting according to the season and lunar cycle. It has
now evolved into a form of psychological profiling.

*Astrology's character descriptions constitute 'the worlds oldest
psychological model and which remains the most widely known form of
personality analysis' 2.*

I'm not going to argue the case for Astrology. I don't have to.
Thousands of millions of people everyday read their stars for all
kinds of different reasons. Some people read their stars for
curiosity's sake, some people read their stars for guidance when
they're feeling low, some people read their stars for inspiration
when things are slack, some people read their stars for confir-
mation of decisions when things are going well and  some for
religious reasons (in some circles it has replaced god). Some
people read their friends' stars to tease someone *('well what do
you expect, he/she is a Sagittarius / Leo / Capricorn!')* and some
people have a quick read of them simply for entertainment.

I am an Astrologer who sees clients in private practice and I
write a column for a parenting magazine. In some ways writing
an Astrological column does a dis-service to Astrology, in that it's
a system of thought that uses philosophy, psychology and an

understanding of human nature to give us a place to contemplate our existence. When it's reduced to a few lines for each sign, it almost seems like cheapening it, or reducing it to its smallest facet.

No-one is born an Astrologer, it comes from years of practice and most people are attracted to the subject, in the early stages, by identifying with those Sun sign profiles. You read how sensitive and psychic Pisces is, or how deep and intense a Scorpio is and you resonate with that concept. You read everything about it and then later on when you learn about the different aspects of your psyche, things seem to fall into place. Well, that's how it was for me.

We are all different and to me, Astrology confirms those differences, defines those varieties, not in a linear fashion, but in a creative, wordy, sometimes seemingly unusual fashion, but define it does.

As there are 12 signs of the Zodiac, 12 signs the Ascendant can be in and 12 signs that the ten planets from the Moon to Pluto can be in, there is enough room for us to identify those differences. *Planet: A celestial body that orbits around the Sun. Star: With the exception of the Moon and the planets, every fixed point of light in the sky is a star, including the Sun. However in Astrology we use the term 'planet' for all the bits we use. So if you catch me calling the Sun, a planet, that is an Astrological term, not one used in astronomy.*

Like my first book *How to Survive a Pisces*, this book is written to help people overcome problems with the people they come across in their lives. After the Pisces book was published, I was asked if I was going to write about the other signs, to which I said 'Yes'. I wanted to work backwards through the Zodiac as I'd started from the wrong end so if you're an Aries, it will take me a while to get to you!

Not too many people have had a negative experience of an Aquarius, well not as many as they might with a Pisces, so this is written to help you learn the *differences* between Aquarians and also what *binds* and *unites* them. And since friendship and bonding are so important to an Aquarian, I shall explain why that is, and how to make the best of any Aquarians you come across.

I have two Aquarian sisters, an Aquarius mother, an Aquarius Auntie (who sadly died while I was writing this book) and an Aquarius ex-mother-in-law, so I can safely say I know a thing or two about the species! But I am the first to admit I don't know everything. How could I? As this book will explain, there are 12 signs their Moon could be in, 12 signs their Ascendant could be in, and if you were to take into account the ten planets we use in Astrology, there are lots of different combinations that this person's chart could possess.....but let me start in an easy place.

I will show you how you can find out the three key things about their chart that will help you understand the Aquarius you know and learn about bonding with them.

Hopefully also in this little book you will learn a thing or two about how to be friends with an Aquarius and what bonding means to them.

Aquarians aren't interested in being Mum, (leave that to Cancerians) but they will want to be brother/sister/friend/Mum to your ideas.

Want to save tigers in Africa? Or free some enslaved beings in a small village? Tell an Aquarius your ideas and they will follow you to the ends of the Earth - because an Aquarius is motivated by ideas. The wackier the better.

Here we have Suzanne, a young mother talking about how her brain works:

*"My brain works differently to most people's - I see an alternative angle, which doesn't always go down well but at least life is never boring."*

So, how do you get an Aquarius on your side?

First of all they need a lot of space. Don't hem them in with restrictions, or rules. You can't affect their minds though. I can safely say that the (average) Aquarius mind is so unique to them, that no amount of badgering or bullying will make them steer away from their basic belief that every man, woman and child is entitled to freedom of ideas.

Now, Aquarians need friends. This is not the same as the friendship demanded by Leos, their opposite sign. Leo friendship is one of needing thanks and praise and reassurance that they are a good person.

Aquarian friendship is a desire to be part of something but also to be separate from it. That sounds perverse I know, but is a fact. An Aquarius wants to think (not feel, that's a Water sign trait) that they are part of something big, but unique within it.

For instance, my mother is a Catholic. She converted when she was in the A.T.S just before the second world war. I asked her why, and she said that the people who she was friends with had 'something' about them: a confidence, a camaraderie that she didn't have. By joining their group, she then felt, sorry, *thought* that she was part of something 'big' (religion) but that she could be unique in her expression of it.

In her case, she has Sun in the 9th house, the house of spirituality, so it made sense that being connected to the wider world of religion was important to her.

Meanwhile my Auntie (her sister) who also converted, did so (according to my mother) because of the rosary beads and all the trimmings of religion. She had her Sun in the 3rd house, Moon in Pisces and a Scorpio Ascendant: this gave her a much more *feeling* take on things.

Both of them became Catholics but only (I believe) as a rebellious take on not complying with my Grandfather, who was a confirmed atheist.

For a fuller account of the history of Astrology, please see my first book *How To Survive a Pisces* or Nick Campion's detailed account of Astrology's beginnings in his two volumes: *The Dawn of Astrology* and *The Golden Age of Astrology*.

We know full well that what the Babylonians saw as planets

travelling through constellations in the sky, is now the sky divided into 12 equal parts and each section is a sign of the Zodiac, the first part being Aries.

It's a bit like the Periodic Table. The different lines and levels of it don't actually exist, but they are just a way of recording the atomic weights of each element in nature. It's a work-in-progress. Astrology is the same. It isn't finite and we discover new things all the time. The movements of the planets going through each sign of the Zodiac are recorded in a publication called an Ephemeris.

That's where the maths comes into it, which is why calculating a horoscope or birth chart is so much easier nowadays. Computers have speeded up the ability to calculate and refine the information.

However, with there being ten planets that we take into account in a chart, making an accurate summary of its potential can be daunting for a beginner, so for the purposes of this book and for simplicity's sake, all we will be concentrating on is three important things: The 'house' the Sun is in, the sign the Moon is in and something called the Ascendant or rising Sign: based on the time of birth.

The Astrology that I practise and that I am talking about only applies to the modern western world. It wouldn't apply in say a village in the Gambia or somewhere where birth records are not kept. You can only make a birth chart and describe a person's character in the West if you have their correct birth data: date, time, location. My cousin's daughter lives in the Gambia and married two local men - neither of whom had any idea when they were born. My Astrology wouldn't help them or be of any use. Their local customs are more relevant.

So let us learn about the sign we are going to bond with.

Mary L English
Bath 2010

*Chapter One*

# The Sign

*"I love them... they are quirky! I gave my Aquarian best friend a pair of mismatching socks for her birthday! For me, they have a charisma."*
A female Pisces

*"It is one of the signs that really intrigues me and never fully understood. I've found the Aquarians I've met to be very difficult to really get to 'know'. The first thing that springs to mind is 'unusual'."*
A female Virgo

## The Sign of Aquarius

Astrology is the study of the planets but not in the astronomical sense. We look at the planets and record where they are from the viewpoint of the earth and we divide the sky into 12 portions, and one of those portions is designated to be the sign of Aquarius. There is no planet called Aquarius, and there isn't infact a star called that either or even a constellation. This is what gets Astronomers hot-under-the-collar because they think Astrologers base their calculations on a set of stars in the sky. Not so. We base our calculations on the equinoxes. Aries being the start of the Astrological year and Libra being the end of summer.

So, who or what is an Aquarius? To call someone an Aquarian, they have to be born between a certain set of dates when the Sun was in the sign of Aquarius. These dates are 21st January to 18th February. However, it does depend on what year the person was born, and their location of birth.

The dates we use can vary from year to year, which is something that confuses quite a lot of people. Please make sure you check with a reputable computer programme or good online resource to ensure that the person you are bonding with actually is an Aquarius... because if you discover after further investigation that your Aquarius is actually a Capricorn or even a Pisces, you'll be working with incorrect information and all the advice I am giving you will be wrong.

Having said that, let's assume for the sake of simplicity that you definitely have an Aquarius in your life. What qualities make them what they are?

The best definition I have found is by Felix Lyle in *The Instant Astrologer* 3. and includes the keywords:

sociable, communicative, altruistic, progressive, independent, rational, detached, eccentric, dogmatic, erratic and cranky.

Here we have the various qualities of their sign veering from the best to the worst. Which qualities has your Aquarius got? I suppose if your Aquarius is your first-born child, all the positive virtues will trip off your lips, but what if your Aquarius is your ex-wife or your employer? Maybe some of the more negative qualities will come to mind and drive you bonkers.

The nice thing about Astrology is, we accept all the signs positive and negative points and it would be daft to say one sign is 'better' than another. The signs are just signs or signals helping us to understand each other.

I know if I meet an Aquarius who has Moon in Leo or a Leo Ascendant, that they will feel better and more understood by me, if I take into account that they like to feel praised. And being thanked goes down really well too.

I find that understanding someone's gestalt, which Astrology allows us to do, makes being with them so much easier.

I would never ask a Gemini for their opinion of something, unless I was prepared to listen. I would also never expect an Aquarius to enjoy a huggy, touchy-feely soul-mate workshop where everyone had to reach into their deepest emotions and act them out for the group... No, they would be far happier accompanying me on a visit to South London to meet a member of the Lesbian Vegan Society who has just exhibited her first transgender Art-work entitled 'Against the Odds' in the local library... Which brings me round neatly to the question of sexuality.

Are all Aquarian women gay? Or even closet gays? I must say I know more gay/lesbian Aquarians than any other sign, but that might be because Aquarians aren't bothered about being gay, when other signs might keep it quieter.

Don't worry though if you're a heterosexual Aquarian, you're included too!

One thing is for sure, Aquarians are constantly described as being different, weird or original, depending on which side of the fence you are sitting. Why is that? Well it's because of Uranus, their ruling planet.

All signs of the Zodiac have been given a planet that looks after them, we call them their 'rulers'. The Sun rules Leo, the Moon rules Cancer and so on...

Well, Aquarius' ruler is now a planet called Uranus. Originally they were ruled by Saturn but Astrologers had to have a re-think when Uranus was discovered. It sort of put an end to the previous system of 12 signs and 7 rulers.

## Uranus

I love Uranus. He's my favourite planet. Funny really considering I'm a Pisces, I ought to have a love for Neptune but I find that too much Neptune stops you getting out of bed and I do like zooming around on my 50cc motor-scooter...

The whole discovery of Uranus sums up the energy of the planet and its reflected expression through Western mankind.

I live in Bath in the West Country of the UK. I moved here soon after my (amicable) divorce. I have been to the Herschel Museum of Astronomy in Bath that is the home place of the birth of the discovery of Uranus. For me it was rather like those shrines you get in Portugal or France. It's almost a religious experience seeing all the little details of the life of William Herschel, a musician and astronomer living in Bath in Georgian times, and his sister Caroline. You can buy a little pamphlet about William Herschel and look at his Astronomy equipment and other more personal things behind glass in cabinets. To report the story so long after the event hardly does it justice but suffice to say William Herschel was a talented man.

He was born in Hanover in Germany in 1738, making him a Scorpio (intense) with Moon in Capricorn (emotionally robust) and started life as an oboist in the Hanoverian Guards. Having been posted to England with the Guards he was so impressed by life there that he moved to the UK to live. After a time he moved to Bath in 1780 and lived with his devoted sister Caroline (Sun Pisces, Moon Cancer, both empathetic and emotionally sensitive signs), and set-up shop as a musician and music teacher.

During the day he entertained the locals with recitals of his own compositions, playing the cello, oboe and organ. But at night be came alive and watched the stars.

He was what could only be described politely as 'an amateur' Astronomer. All the same Uranus was discovered by him (or some say by Caroline).

There was William an Astronomical geek, looking through his telescope at night, tracking the path of one planet in particular. He experimented with telescopic lenses and developed a lens that meant he could see further into space and track the movements of planets no-one would have been capable of before. Without this extra strong lens he never would have seen the planet at all.

Although William was an amateur Astronomer, his discoveries and technical achievements had a big impact at the time. His ambition was to extend telescopic vision into space by increasing the size of the actual telescopes.

Although he is best remembered for the discovery of Uranus,

William was also responsible for increasing the dimensions of the Milky Way, discovering the satellites of Saturn and other planets, the rotation of Saturn's rings, as well as the motion of binary stars. Through his observations of the Sun, William accidentally discovered the existence of infra-red radiation. Using thermometers and prisms he conducted experiments which led to a series of papers being published in 1800 on the discovery of the independent behaviour of radiant heat and visible light.

During the time he lived at 19 New King Street, Bath, William experimented with techniques for grinding and polishing specula mirrors. In 1789 he completed work on what was then, the world's largest telescope which was a reflector, 40 feet in length with a massive 48 inch mirror which proved very problematic to cast and polish.

It was built and used in the gardens of Observatory House, Slough, which is where it stayed until it was destroyed in a gale in 1839.

## The Astronomer and the King

King George III had a fascination for science, and Astronomy in particular. He kept abreast of the latest discoveries and patronised the leading astronomers of the day. When William Herschel made his discovery of Uranus in 1781, his fame quickly spread and the King was duly impressed. This led to a royal appointment and a grant of £200 a year to further his research at the King's seat, Datchet, near Windsor, and latterly at Slough.

In return he was expected to show the Royal Family and their guests interesting astronomical observations. Later the King rewarded Herschel with £4,000 towards the construction of his 40ft telescope as well as a generous payment of £50 per year for his sister Caroline.

The planet Uranus was first seen in the night sky in 1690 by John Flamsteed, but he thought it was a star. He catalogued it and called it '34 Tauri.'

William Heschel observed it and understood that it was *not* a star and named it the 'Georgian Planet' in honour of his patron, King George III. Others at that time called the planet Herschel after the man who discovered it.

## Supreme God of the Heavens

As most of the previous planetary discoveries had been named after ancient gods from Greek mythology, the name Uranus came into common use around 1850.

Uranus was the god of the heavens. He was the earliest supreme god.

In the Olympian creation myth, Uranus came every single night to cover the Earth and mate with Gaia, the Earth goddess, but he hated the children she bore him and imprisoned Gaia's youngest children in Tartarus; a deep, gloomy place, a pit, or an abyss used as a dungeon of torment and suffering that resides beneath the underworld.

To facilitate her revenge for imprisoning her children, Gaia shaped a great flint sickle and asked her sons to castrate Uranus. Only Cronus (Saturn) was willing to do it: he ambushed his father and castrated him, casting the severed parts into the sea, which gave birth to the lovely goddess Aphrodite, rising from the sea foam.

From the blood which spilled from Uranus onto the Earth came forth the Gigantes, the three snake-haired avenging Furies. After his castration, the Sky no longer came to cover the Earth at night, but stayed up above.

The astrological community then had to make a correlation between the activity of Uranus and the Western population and it was decided, after much argument and discussion, that Uranus would 'rule' the star sign Aquarius.

I am very lucky to live in the city where Uranus was discovered and I have viewed the exhibits in the museum many times. I sometimes feel a little like a spy walking around as

Astrology is now so distant from Astronomy. In fact you'd barely know they were once sisters. Today the paths of Astrology and Astronomy have diverged. Astronomy went on to become a 'science' and Astrology has become a sort of pagan belief system, maybe nearer to its early roots. Doesn't bother me. We can have plenty of fun without being a 'science'....

In Astronomy, Uranus takes 84 years to circle the Sun. Its orbit is strange and involves tilting at almost 98%. In Astrology it takes 84 years for Uranus to make a complete circuit of the birth-chart, so you will have to reach that age to see your 'Uranus Return'.

The keywords we use to describe Uranus are: freedom, individuality, ideas and suddenness. And it is known as the 'ruler' of Aquarius, which I consider to be a fitting choice. As Howard Sasportas notes: "Uranus timed its entrance with flair, to coincide with three major social revolutions also intent on disrupting the established order of things. The American and French revolutions and the advent of the Industrial Revolution." 4.

There are a lot of Aquarians who practice Astrology. Almost as many as Pisceans. Pisceans are more likely to enjoy Astrology because it gives some *feeling* of connection while Aquarians enjoy the *idea* of connection.

Remember: Aquarius energy is light, cerebral, inconsistent and erratic.

I will now explain the six most important concepts that motivate an Aquarius. They are friendship, individuality, freedom, differentness, uniqueness and new ideas.

## Friendship

You really can't beat a dictionary definition when describing a word and a 'friend' is a 'person with whom one enjoys mutual affection and regard, sympathiser, helper, someone who is not an enemy'.

Aquarians find it hard to live without friendship. It's their motivating factor. An Aquarius friend will meet you and want to experience something with you depending on their Moon sign and other chart factors.They mostly can manage on their own. Unlike other signs who need partners to feel complete or whole, as a general rule Aquarius can exist quite happily by themselves. However, to deprive an Aquarius of friendship would be the biggest form of torture of all.

And they are very hot on humanitarian issues too: the planet and the freedom of the population.

Carol is an Aquarius who has worked in a University and now lives in the country with her husband and pet cats. She works locally with people with learning difficulties and describes why she does this:

*"I teach students with severe learning difficulties and love it, it feels to be an extension of my strong views on defending human rights: life long active member of Amnesty."*

Here her friendship extends to helping others be empowered. That's not to say that Aquarians necessarily want to lead people, more a case of being inspired by their ideals. Leaders are more Aries material.

The need for friendship can start in early life. The famous British musician Jacqueline du Pre led a whirlwind existence in the classical musical industry as a cellist until her untimely early death aged 42 from M.S. Before all the fame and as a young child,when asked what she wanted for her birthday, the ten-year-old Jacqueline du Pre replied, "a friend".

Friendship runs through the lives of most of the famous people I have quoted in this book.

Actor Paul Newman was friends with the playwright, novelist and biographer A E Hotchner age 91 for more than 50 years. Paul was an Aquarius with Moon in softy Pisces and Aaron is a Cancer with Moon in bountiful Sagittarius. They founded together the company 'Newman's Own' that produced food items (a very Cancer type of work) and started with salad dressings they made at home. All profits from the company were given to good causes in true Aquarian style.

Paul said: *"My profits will be divided between a number of tax-deductible charities and causes, some church-related, others for conservation and ecology and things like that."*.They used to go fishing together and kept in contact the whole of Paul's life.

After Paul's death headlines from the New York Times in September 2008 read: "Newman Remembered as a Good Neighbor and a Good Friend".

There are extremes of friendship too. Sometimes it's fluffy and light-hearted, sometimes it's dark and doomy. But to identify an Aquarius and understand them fully, you have to grasp how important friendship is to them.

In January 2009 the socialite Paris Hilton starred in a reality TV show called 'British Best Friend' where contestants competed to become Paris' best friend. This started as a show in the USA called My New Best Friend Forever. Contestants had to take part in weird assessments and tasks like going to an all night party, designing a dress for Paris, visiting a farm to see if they like animals as much as Paris and then performing in a talent show. When asked in an interview what the contestants were doing to impress her in the show Paris said: "I like it when they're having fun and not being desperate hungry tigers. I don't like it when people act so hungry and weird." So, to be Paris' friend, forget about feelings and emotions!

This is at the extreme end of the friendship axis with Abraham Lincoln the 16th president of the USA at the other end saying things like:

*"A friend is one who has the same enemies as you have"* and *"Am I not destroying my enemies when I make friends of them?"*

There are also various concerns about where friendship will lead.

Two famous Aquarians fell foul of revealing too much to interested outsiders.

Germaine Greer the Australian academic writer and journalist complained: *"I decided that henceforth I would never read any account of myself whether flattering or otherwise, and no friends who used me as grist to their mill would remain friends."*

Actress Charlotte Rampling hired lawyers to try to block the publication of a biography about her written by a 'close friend' when it revealed more than she wanted to about her personal life. Her argument was it would upset her children. It transpired that this wasn't a friendship at all, but a working relationship that turned sour.

I especially loved Virginia Woolf's comment *"I have lost friends, some by death... others through sheer inability to cross the street."*

Of course with the internet their community and friendships can be instantaneous and global. But with no access to friends or clubs or societies or groups or online community, Aquarians will fade away.

Carol who I mentioned earlier has Moon in Gemini and commented: *"I like groups though I like to dip in an out of them."*

Aquarians like to think they are a small cog in a big wheel. Part of something. Joined by an interest, idea or conviction.

For example, they may join the National Trust. Not because of the history (that's Capricorn's department) but because their membership makes them feel they belong to something bigger and if they have a friend who is a member, better still.

## Green Parents

Mother of two, Melissa is passionate about green issues and natural parenting. Feeling frustrated at the lack of inspirational parenting magazines on the shelves she launched a magazine for local Brighton parents after the birth of her second daughter. Reader response was so positive that the magazine became national in 2004, and international in 2005. When faced with a little relaxation time, Melissa chooses to take a walk in the woods, read a book, do some yoga or celebrate any occasion with friends, delicious food and good wine.

This describes the editor/owner of The Green Parent Magazine and is a classic example of an Aquarius. She created a magazine to unite other mothers to the suffering of the planet. Melissa is an Aquarian with a Capricorn Ascendant (serious and deter-minded), Sun in the 2nd house (of things we value), and Moon in Scorpio (which gives her focus and insightfulness).

Teamed with her Pisces husband, she has achieved her goal of making new friends who think the same way as her. It's not a fashion statement. It's fuelled by a genuine desire to unite people for one cause. She's the boss so that preserves her freedom, and the magazine has lots of readers which assists the friendship element of her sign.

To bond with an Aquarius you first have to understand their motivations. What makes them tick, the breath that keeps them alive. Each Aquarius will have a different life-view: represented by the Ascendant, a different home: the house their Sun is in, and a different way of dealing with emotions: influenced by the sign of the Moon. But underneath all of this is the unchanging gestalt that they are a member of the human race working towards being with other like-minded people.

They can have lots of friends or one or two but they must have friends so if you want to bond and be friends with an Aquarius you will need to have your 'interesting-person' hat on.

## Individuality

Thomas Moore makes a great case for individuality in his book *Soul Mates*. He argues that you can't have individuality, without having a sense of community. The two go hand in hand:

*"While soul is what allows us to make intimate connections and so*

*create community-even a global and universal sense of shared life-it is also responsible for our most profound sense of individuality and uniqueness. These two-community and individuality-go together. You can't have genuine community unless it consists of true individuals, and you can't be an individual unless you are deeply involved in community"* 5.

So I asked a few Aquarians I know to give me their views on individuality and here are their replies:

### Female, Libra Ascendant, Sun in the 5<sup>th,</sup> Moon in Aquarius

With her Libra Ascendant, Karmini is focused on personal relationships and fairness and is happily re-married. She lives in a small village and has three children, the youngest of which is home-educated. She is an Artist/Creator and has her own studio which is in keeping with hrt Sun in the 5<sup>th</sup> . With her Moon also in Aquarius she also enjoys being part of various groups including a women's group and treasurer to the local forest school group.

*"Vital and exciting, someone described as this would get me very interested in them, I would want to meet them; possibly feel I had something in common with them. I like the idea that people who are individual will think for themselves and that I would find them interesting."*

### Female, Scorpio Ascendant, Sun in the 3<sup>rd</sup>, Moon in Libra

Suzanne also lives in a small village and helps run a complementary health school. She is married and also has three children. With her Scorpio Ascendant she takes time to trust people but her Sun in the 3<sup>rd</sup> house helps make her good at conversing and engaging. With her Moon in Libra she's heavily into relationships and frets if her partner seems unhappy.

*"Individuality comes easily and just seems to 'be' Aquarius. I don't mind being different, I consider myself different as in slightly off the*

*norm and certainly I have several friends who are Aquarians and they are the most 'individual' amongst my friends. My closest friends are all highly individual and most of them are born within 6 weeks of me on the astrological chart. Aquarians seem to really enjoy the freedom of the journey, both metaphorically and literally."*

## Male, Virgo Ascendant, Sun in the 6<sup>th</sup>, Moon in Cancer

Nkera left his life in the business world and re-trained as a massage therapist. With a Virgo Ascendant he's interested in health and healing and with his Sun in the 6<sup>th</sup> this is amplified. His Moon is in Cancer which brings out his nurturing side.

*"Everyone is an individual... but some are more individual than others!"*

## Female, Capricorn Ascendant, Sun in the 2<sup>nd</sup>, Moon in Scorpio

Green Parent Melissa joins the others in her views on being an individual.

*"Individuality is really important to me and has been from a young age. I have always valued my individuality and made a statement about it as a teenager wearing weird customised clothes and dying my hair crazy colours. Now I'm in my thirties I feel very content in my own skin and am aware that I often look, feel and think differently from the crowd."*

So, to bond with your Aquarius, you will need to be sure that you're not influenced others and that you're a person in your own right.

## Freedom

The definition of freedom for an Aquarius is as follows. As they are ruled by the planet Uranus - who Astrologers have deemed is the planet of freedom - their sense of freedom is 'freedom to be different', to not be the same as everyone else. Freedom is also defined as not being told what to do. Now the nature of humans I suppose you could say is that we all like to feel free, so what makes an Aquarius so concerned with this issue?

I asked some Aquarians for their definition of freedom and here are their replies:

### Female, Libra Ascendant, Sun in the 5th, Moon in Aquarius

Here's Karmini our Artist/Creator again:

*"Freedom is a must in my life and what I always seem to be striving for and searching for. I can feel very frustrated and rebellious by not having freedom and choice in any aspect in my life. I feel I am always on the watch to avoid getting hemmed in by bureaucracy, responsibilities and other people's expectations."*

### Female, Scorpio Ascendant, Sun 3rd, Moon in Libra

Suzanne has this point of view on freedom:

*"Freedom, ties into friends for me. I have lots of peripheral friends, from all walks of life, but only a handful of close friends. I don't like being tied down by needy people, I seem to become smothered in friendships and I literally wilt."*

### Male, Virgo Ascendant, Sun in the 6th, Moon in Cancer

Here Nkera gives his view of what freedom means for him:

*"I've always tried to be free to do things in my own way and think the way I want and I usually manage to do both much to the shock of others around me."*

### Female, Capricorn Ascendant, Sun in the 2nd, Moon in Scorpio

Melissa enjoys most of the Summer months in a yurt in her garden, runs her own business with her husband and brings her children up with an awareness of nature.

*"Freedom is hugely important to me. I always remember the maxim 'If you love someone, set them free.' I aim for a high degree of freedom in my life. I also want my children to experience a real freedom in childhood with the knowledge that I have set boundaries and am holding the space for them, so that they feel safe."*

## Liberation

Oprah Winfrey donated $1 million and pledged her support for the National Underground Railroad Freedom Center, Cincinnati, Ohio, a museum educating visitors about the secret network of escape routes that came to be called "the Underground Railroad" that liberated slaves from the south of America. This is a classic example of something that would appeal to an Aquarius, which is Oprah's Sun sign.

First of all the concept of slavery would not go down well with an Aquarius. Secondly the fact that a host of people managed to liberate those slaves, by working together would certainly get an Aquarian's attention.

## Differentness

Another key phrase for Aquarius is 'being different'. Back to the dictionary for a definition of different which tells us that it means: 'unlike, of other nature, form or quality, separate, distinct and unusual'. Again I asked some Aquarians for their views.

### Female, Scorpio Ascendant, Sun in the 3rd, Moon in Libra
Suzanne again:

*"I don't seem to see things quite the same way as other people and I don't mind. What other people see as an obstacle, I'll see as a challenge. I guess everyone is unique, but Aquarians don't fit the mould, they never have - they've always been on a slightly different wavelength (planet some might say) and often interpret things differently to most. I know this can be challenging for some people, I and indeed most of my Aquarian friends can seem aloof, but it's not that at all, it's just us being in our own space and time - we don't conform easily and aren't that easy to predict – it's not a conscious or rebellious thing, it just IS!*

*I sometimes have to pull myself back to the here and now as my mind is out there thinking of something else, from tomorrow's dinner to the correctness of torture methods used when interro-*

*gating prisoners. I can and do switch around like this often – sometimes I can hear the clanking in my brain and I think people must think I'm a bit dim as it takes me a while to come back to the current subject and answer the question posed."*

## Female, Libra Ascendant, Sun 5th, Moon Aquarius

Karmini here describes how being different makes her interested. She struggled a bit when one of her children wanted to go back into mainstream education but got round it by thinking about alternative further education:

*"'How interesting this sounds'; 'I want to know more'. I like the idea of being different myself but when I look at my life and some of the things I do I can worry that other people must think I am quite odd! But it doesn't change me - I just think about it. I sometimes have to watch that I am not being different for being different's sake; for example, we home educate our children and joined a small parent run school. It did work and brought lots of lovely things, but I also found that I did have to look carefully and make sure that this did work for the children too - it ticked my box but I have to accept that particularly as they have got older, that they may want to be like everybody else and go to a mainstream school. Our eldest has just done this and it is fine; as long as he is happy I find I can go along with it. However, I have already thought of Further Education that will be different to the run of the mill!"*

## Male, Virgo Ascendant, Sun in the 6th, Moon in Cancer

When answering this question you can see Nkera isn't just answering it in a standard way:

*"As long as I can remember, I have always been different. Other people tell me I'm different. I often feel different, sometimes I want to be different and even enjoy it. Sometimes I wonder how I ended up this different, but strangely, sometimes I'm not that different after all and I understand exactly what everyone is all about 'cos they're just like me and I'm just like them and it's great just*

*watching the world go by just like a giant TV screen, but then why can't I pull them out of the TV screen?"*

## Female, Capricorn Ascendant, Sun in the 2nd, Moon in Scorpio

Melissa likes the idea of being different and her Moon in Scorpio likes the concept of deepness, a very Scorpio trait:

*"Hmm - always have felt a bit different, a bit 'weird' but I have mostly enjoyed that feeling of being on the outside looking in. Or sometimes, being on the outside, looking deeper outside! I remember starting a diary aged 11 and writing "People think I'm a bit weird but I don't mind. I like that."*

Now there is a connection between 'different' and 'weird'. Ask ten people their definition of weirdness and I'm sure they'll come up with quite a few answers but the summary would be 'doing things that other people don't do' i.e. not following the norm. Actress Charlotte Rampling said "To discover what normal means, you have to surf a tide of weirdness."

And that weirdness or differentness can manifest in other ways. Here we have an Aquarius talking about the old and the new in her life. She owns certain things that are old and 'different' but she also owns things that are modern and 'different'. As it stands at the moment, not many people have solar panels, maybe in the future when everyone has them, Aquarians will stop wanting them!

## Female, Cancer Ascendant, Sun 7th, Moon in Gemini

Carol is married to and lives with her Cancer husband and two cats. She now cares for her elderly parents.

*"I like sci-fi even though it's supposed to be nerdy. I used to like caving - something a bit different and also lots of 'journeys'. I like old things. I like old machines - like an ancient hand-worked Singer sewing machine and an old Clocking-in clock. I have a house that is part 1820-part 1971 and that suits me down to the ground. I have*

*an actual wood burning oven that I use quite a bit, sat opposite a conventional electric oven. I have solar panels too. And a computer."*

Carol describes how some of the things she owns are antique, which keeps her Cancer Ascendant happy and other things are modern which fits in nicely with her Sun sign Aquarius and her quirkiness shines through with her love of sci-fi.

It's not that Aquarians purposefully aim for being different but because they think in a non-linear manner, this just happens.

## Uniqueness

The dictionary definition of unique is: 'being the only one of its kind, having no like or equal or parallel, unusual'. Now you could quite rightly say that everyone is unique, which they are, but Aquarians strive to resonate on a personal unique frequency. They will surround themselves with people, ideas or things that are unique. So, if you said to an Aquarian: 'everyone is doing so-and-so' they'd just look the other way. But if you said something and/or planned something that they hadn't heard about, they'd want to know more. My mother is always suggesting things that are completely off-centre. I've got used to it now but to outsiders it can seem completely wacky.

Once again I asked some real Aquarians for their views.

### Female, Libra Ascendant, Sun 5th, Moon Aquarius

Karmini certainly lives an unusual life. She spent 5 years being a La Leche League breast-feeding counsellor and now hosts days for women friends in her studio so they can restore some area of creativity in their lives.

*"Wonderful, just one of kind! It is what I would like to be described as. It has quite a magical quality to it - no-one and nothing else like it in the world. I find it very exciting."*

Both Nkera and Melissa rightly point out that everyone is unique but then go onto explain their viewpoints

**Male, Virgo Ascendant, Sun in the 6ᵗʰ, Moon in Cancer**
Nkera:

> *"Everyone is unique. Strange how some spend so much effort trying to be someone else and some spend so much energy trying to make others be just like them!!"*

**Female, Capricorn Ascendant, Sun in the 2ⁿᵈ, Moon in Scorpio**
Melissa:

> *"Everyone is unique. I love discovering more about people. I love those conversations that really establish a connection. I really enjoy exploring other people's thoughts and opinions."*

Notice how these Aquarians are excited by thoughts, opinions and ideas.

## New Ideas

> *"To make ideas effective, we must be able to fire them off."*
> Virginia Woolf, Moon in Aries

Ideas are the life-blood of all the Air signs; Gemini, Libra and Aquarius. They live and breathe them. An idea is a 'plan or scheme formed by thinking, mental impression or conception', and for an Aquarius *new* ideas are even more exciting. Now this is something that the Earth signs find difficult to understand and the Water signs just don't connect to. An Earth sign would wonder why they need to do things differently, what all the fuss is about. The Water signs observe all the goings on and generally ignore things until it affects their feelings. The Fire signs however, get caught up in the general ideas-making and run with things, until they get exhausted. An Air sign can have millions of ideas, on and on. It's their way of life.

I then asked my Aquarian volunteers to expand a bit on their views of ideas. This really sparked them off, as you can see below.

**Female, Libra Ascendant, Sun 5th, Moon Aquarius**
Karmini tells us about her own ideas for doing things in a better way:

*"I am not so stimulated by other people's new ideas but often find myself inventing things in my mind - a better way, a new way to do something. For instance I know that in the not too distant future DVDs, videos etc will disappear and we will be able to access absolutely anything we want to watch from a film/programme database through our TV remote controls. We will be able to 'search' (just as we do on computers) for old programmes, documentaries, foreign films. We will pay according to what we watch and will be charged through a credit card or something like that. I also had the idea some time ago, of a car windscreen that was rain sensitive, so that you didn't have to turn them on yourself. They would come on when the rain started and go at the appropriate speed for the amount of rain. BMW I believe have already done this and may be some other cars too by now. With ideas I can find myself torn between wanting progress but also wanting to hold on to the human-ness of what we do at the moment or in the past. I don't really relish the idea of an automated world - in fact I don't like it at all, but I do find myself coming up with ideas that are going in that direction!"*

**Male, Virgo Ascendant, Sun in the 6th, Moon in Cancer**
Nkera went through a major life-change by becoming a therapist his 'good idea'. He's much happier now.

*"Love em.... just wish I had more of them. Seems like they used to flow more readily when I was younger....then I took one responsibility....then another....and another.....and almost got lost, but then*

*the light came on again......welcome back, me!"*

## Male Aquarius on a dating website
*"Heaven for me is long, slow, intimate conversations with lots of careful listening and no assumptions or jumping to conclusions - the sense of really getting to know someone, being known, and exploring experiences and ideas."*

## Female, Capricorn Ascendant, Sun in the 2nd, Moon in Scorpio
Melissa has to have ideas to keep her magazine feeling fresh.
*"24/7 - my mind is often on hyperdrive, buzzing with new ideas, plans and projects. I love planning new ideas. As I get older it's getting easier for me to stick with just a few projects but I do feel a need to keep growing and expanding my knowledge continuously. Many of my friends think of my house as a library where they can find books on anything from permaculture to the ancient Maya, positive parenting to sacred sex."*

## Female, Scorpio Ascendant, Sun in the 3rd, Moon in Libra
*"New ideas - I have these all the time, usually they are theories, concepts, philosophising - I'm not that interested in seeing them come to fruition, as a mother though, this is an excellent skill to have up your sleeves when being with children."*

Suzanne makes a valid point here. She says her ideas don't have to actually lead anywhere. This is something I learned about my Mum only in her later life. I thought every time she had an idea, we all had to follow suit or encourage her, or 'do' whatever she suggested. No, she just has to 'have' the idea and think about it and I just have to say to her 'good idea' and she's happy. Sometimes making the idea a reality takes the enjoyment out of it
.

## Female, Cancer Ascendant, Sun 7th, Moon in Gemini
Carol found that places of intense study seemed to produce the

most amount of ideas and was where she felt happiest.

*"I like ideas. Universities are the nicest places I have worked."*

If you could follow an Aquarian's thoughts for one day, you'd be shocked. There is so much going on! How do they ever have time to eat.....or sleep?

If you want a fabulous example of Aquarian thinking, then read anything by Virginia Woolf. She describes her thinking process wonderfully. She had a Gemini Ascendant which gave her the ability to communicate well, but her Sun was in the 8$^{th}$ house so she got obsessed with some of the darker sides of the psyche too, and with her Moon in Aries she could also get very cross about things.

*"My own brain is to me the most unaccountable of machinery - always buzzing, humming, soaring roaring diving, and then buried in mud. And why? What's this passion for?" Virginia Woolf*

*Chapter Two*

# How To Make A Chart

As this is a book about how to easily identify the sort of Aquarius that is in your life, I will explain the three most important things you need to know, how to get that information and what to do with it after you've discovered it.

These days it is really easy to make a birth chart. There are numerous online resources to make one. But the common cry is: "What does it all *mean?*"

Luckily you won't have to get a degree or letters after your name or spend hours on the Internet surfing loads of sites to get that answer.

The three pieces of information you need are:

What sign the Ascendant is in
What house the Sun is in and
What sign the Moon is in.

That's enough Astrological information to enable you to under-stand most people and be able to feel you know a little about their characteristics, and in this book's case, how to bond with them. There is, of course, lots of other information you can get from a birth chart and there are ten planets in total which we use in a consultation. However all you need for now is where the Sun is, the sign of the Ascendant and the sign of the Moon.

Opposite is the chart of one of my clients.

She has a Scorpio Ascendant, Sun in the 4th house and Moon in Aquarius. So a quick synopsis would be that she's more likely to play her cards close to her chest and want privacy. Scorpio

Name: ♀ Aquarius Client
born on: Mo. 18 Feb. 1985
in: Ashford, ENG (UK)
0w27, 51n26
Natal Chart (Method: Web Style / equal)
Sun sign: Aquarius
Ascendant: Scorpio

Time:     1:30 am
Univ.Time: 1:30
Sid. Time: 11:20:03

Type 2 GW  0.0.1  22-Mrz-2010

Ascendant doesn't like being the centre of attention (unlike Leo Ascendant) so she'd feel better working in the background. Her Sun is in the 4th house, so her home, nurturing, families, Mum, are all important to her. Her Sun and her Moon are also in Aquarius so emotionally she can distance herself from things if they get too heated.

To make a quick analysis of a chart we only need three peices of information. The **sign** of the **Ascendant**, the **sign** the **Moon** is in and the **house** the **Sun** is in.

This is the abbreviation for the Ascendant:

AC

This is the symbol for the Sun:

This is the symbol for the Moon:

☾

The houses are numbered 1-12 in an anti-clockwise order.

These are the shapes representing the signs, so find the one that matches yours. They are called glyphs.

Aries ♈
Taurus ♉
Gemini ♊
Cancer ♋
Leo ♌
Virgo ♍
Libra ♎
Scorpio ♏
Sagittarius ♐
Capricorn ♑
Aquarius ♒
Pisces ♓

To make your Aquarius chart, go to www.astro.com and make an account then go to the free horoscopes section and scroll down and use the special part of their site, the 'Extended Chart Selection.'

You've already inputted all your data. Under the section marked 'Options', it will say 'House System'. Now *make sure you change the box to say equal-house.* The default system is Placidus and all the houses will be different sizes and for a beginner that's just too confusing.

Your chosen chart will look something like this.

The lines in the centre of the chart are either easy or challenging mathematical associations between each planet in the chart, so ignore them too.

We only want 3 pieces of information. The **sign** of the **Ascendant**, the **sign** the **Moon** is in and the **house** the **Sun** is in.

## The Elements

To understand your Aquarius fully, you must take into account which Element their Ascendant and Moon are in.

Each sign of the Zodiac has been given an element that it operates under : Earth, Air, Fire and Water. I like to think of them as operating at different 'speeds'.

The **Earth** signs are **Taurus**, **Virgo** and **Capricorn**. The Earth Element is stable, grounded and concerned with practical matters. An Aquarius with a lot of Earth in their chart works best at a slow, steady speed. ( I refer to these in the text as 'Earthy').

The **Air** signs are **Gemini**, **Libra** and our friend **Aquarius** (who is the 'Water-carrier' *not* a water sign). The Air element

31

enjoys ideas, concepts and thoughts. It operates at a faster speed than Earth, not as fast as Fire but faster than Water and Earth. Imagine them as being medium speed.

The **Fire** signs are **Aries, Leo** and **Sagittarius**. The Fire element likes action, excitement and can be very impatient. Their speed is *very* fast.( I refer to these as Firey i.e. Fire-Sign).

The **Water** signs are **Cancer, Scorpio** and **Pisces**. The Water element involves feelings, impressions, hunches and intuition. They operate faster than Earth but not as fast as Air. A sort of slow-medium speed.

# Chapter Three

# The Ascendant

Name: ♀ Oprah Winfrey
born on: Fr, 29 Jan 1954
in: Kosciusko, MS (US)
89w35, 33n03
Natal Chart (Method: Web Style / equal)
Sun sign: Aquarius
Ascendant: Sagittarius

Time:        4:30 am
Univ.Time: 10:30
Sid. Time:  13:04:14

ASTRO DIENST
www.astro.com

Type: 2 GW  0.0-1  22-Mrz-2010

This is the birth chart of Oprah Winfrey. Oprah has a Sagittarius Ascendant. She has a great way with people, she will say and do what she likes, and maybe will even put her foot in it occasionally, but because she is such good fun, nobody really minds.

So here are all the Ascendants combined with an Aquarius Sun.

## Aries Ascendant

*"Playing lifts you out of yourself into a deliriously fun place."*
Jacqueline du Pré, Sun in 10<sup>th</sup> house

Jacqueline du Pré, Sun in 10th house

The Aries Ascendant, ruled by Mars, God of War makes the Aquarius a little more confident, a little more self-assured. It's a Fire sign Ascendant and as such makes their view of the world upbeat, dynamic and active. It's a fast energy and one that wants 'me' to be in the picture. They are quick on the draw, quick to include themselves and contribute.

## Taurus Ascendant
*"The prospect of going home is very appealing."*
David Ginola, Sun in 9th house

Taurus is a practical, earthy sign. The Ascendant in this sign talks about practical, graspable concepts. They want things at a slower pace, basic, tangeable and attainable. As Taurus is ruled by Venus the Goddess of Love, issues to do with relationships, love and sex all come to mind. They are in touch with their bodies, their dinners and who they will sleep with at night.

## Gemini Ascendant
*"I suppose our main interest and topic of conversation was who was going out with who."*
Jean English (my mother in her memoirs: 'A Vanished World'.), Sun in 9th house

Gemini loves to chat, to communicate, to take part, be with people, be around *ideas*. Another Air cerebral energy as an Aquarius with a Gemini Ascendant will want to talk things over, not in depth but enough to make their mind buzz with ideas. All the Air signs live by their ideas. With this combination you will have someone who is light, happy and wanting interesting things to discuss and muse over.

## Cancer Ascendant
*"I have no family and that was not intentional and is a cause of a lot*

*of sadness. I have very ill elderly relatives which I have to maintain
and the stress causes me further sadness."*
Female Client C, Sun in 7th house

Cancer Ascendant concerns itself with the family, the home,
children, the things we have to care for. This can include animals
too. It's a water sign and wants to nurture, care, feel empathy for
others but as this is the Water Ascendant of a cerebral Air sign it
makes the Aquarius a little confused sometimes, because on the
one hand they want all the independence that their Sun sign
gives them and they also want the snuggly, familiar things that
makes them feel comfortable....so you could say they want to be
comfortably independent.

## Leo Ascendant

*"I'm a born entertainer, when I open the fridge and the light comes
on, I burst into song."*
Robbie Williams, Sun in 7th house

This is the Aquarius that you will notice. The Firey Leo
Ascendant makes them confident, worried about appearances,
wanting the famous red-carpet to be laid before their feet. They
will want to 'shine', as anything to do with Leo is about needing
recognition for their existence. Words like proud, self-confident,
demonstrative come to mind. So again there is a conflict as
Aquarius is all about not being *noticed* but being *included*. So you
could say here that they want recognition for that inclusion.

## Virgo Ascendant

*"I have devoted so much energy to reach the top that I accept the
stress of being there."*
Placido Domingo, Sun in 5th house

Virgo is an earth sign and as such wants material needs met. It is also the sign that governs health, healing and detail. Dotting the i's and crossing the t's comes naturally to this combination. It's a good sign for worrying and can make the Aquarius fretful about just about everything. They might nurse or care for people, anything that takes health into account. As an Earth sign this Aquarius will be a little more grounded than others provided they feel well.

## Libra Ascendant

*"I had a wife, two children, two dogs, and the next day I didn't have anything."*
Phil Collins, Sun in 4th house

Here we have the sign that wants to relate to others on a more personal level. They feel better when they're in a close, personal relationship (one that gives them freedom to be individual) but relate they must. Airy Libra is also ruled by Venus so again the love thing comes into play. They can be charming, discerning, and like to be surrounded by 'pretty' or 'nice' things. Their homes are more likely to be attractive with a number of pleasing objects on display and they can shy away from arguments and discord.

## Scorpio Ascendant

*"I don't like being tied down by needy people."*
Female Client E, Sun in 3rd house

The Watery Scorpio Ascendant is a more in-depth energy. It's been described as the microscope of attention. The needing to get deeply into something (or someone) wanting to travel to the centre of whatever is going on. Subterranean...If you think of pot-holing you won't go wrong. This is not a light and fluffy energy. To some it may seem intense; to others it will feel faithful and loyal. My Auntie had this and she either loved you, or hated you, there was no in-between...I found a fantastic forum on the internet called 'I'm an Aquarius With Scorpio Rising. Join an anonymous group with personal stories, support group forums, and experiences.' It was the 'anonymous' category that got me chuckling..

## Sagittarius Ascendant

*"When Paris has to pee, Paris has to pee!"*
Paris Hilton, Sun in 3rd houe

So many famous Aquarius people have this Firey Ascendant. Oprah Winfrey, Paris Hilton, Charles Darwin, Lewis Carroll, to name but a few. It helps them do what they want without fear of reprisal or ridicule. It's ruled by upbeat, benevolent Jupiter the God of Gods. Wanting to take you to the highest plane...then dropping you into the dirt when he's tired of you. They'll say it as they see it, speak their minds and are less likely to delay in pushing for new vistas. Jupiter also rules philosophy so this is the Aquarius who will fill you full of their religious or spiritual ideas and will want you to join hands with them for the philosophical party of a lifetime.

## Capricorn Ascendant

*"My mouth is full of decayed teeth and my soul of decayed ambitions."*
James Joyce, Sun in 2nd house

Now the energies slow down again. Back to an Earth sign. Capricorn is the sign of realism in all its forms. Reality is the key word. Hard knocks aren't far off either. Death, delay, darkness on a bad day, wry humour on a good day. Saturn their ruling planet puts the brakes on and helps them see things with no rose tint to their specs. If you want a reality check, ask a Capricorn Ascendant. You'll get it.

## Aquarius Ascendant

*"As our case is new, we must think and act anew."*
Abraham Lincoln, Sun in 1st house

We now come to epitome of Aquarian-ness. Not only are they individual and different but they are fuled by a desire to attain it at all costs. Keep your distance, watch their uniqueness at work, wonder at the ability to see things in a way you can't. Think of Abraham Lincoln. He abolished slavery at a time when it was in full flow and he worked against the prevailing trends with his bigger 'vision'. In a domestic modern-day setting your Aquarius with this Ascendant will want to feel free and for you to join them in that freedom.

## Pisces Ascendant

*"I can think of some things that would be fun, but I'm living my dreams."*
Mike Farrell, Sun in 12th house

This is the most sensitive sign of the Zodiac, so your Aquarius with this Ascendant will detect a drop of angel dust falling on their shoulder, feel you crying thousands of miles away, seem dreamy and mystical and away with the fairies. Hold on though, all is not lost. If they have their Sun in the 11th, there is hope. If they have Sun in the 12th then they are an Aquarius that is masquerading as a Pisces and will need gentle handling, time alone and a peaceful, quiet environment.

(See How to Survive a Pisces for more ideas)

*Chapter Four*

# The Moon

In Astrology the Moon is where we hide. Where we feel things. If the Sun is our conscious self, our Moon is our subconscious and it's always a good idea to keep in touch with the subconscious because without a grasp of its needs we can work 'against' ourselves. Say for instance you are a Gemini and you want to change jobs but you've got your Moon in Taurus.

One part of you will be excited about the prospect of the new horizons appearing before you, while the other part of you will be worried about paying the bills and losing the security of the pension you might have paid into or your favourite mug in the canteen being lost to someone else. It doesn't have to be a dilemma.

Once you discover the sign your Moon is in, or for the purposes of this book found the sign your Aquarian's Moon is in, then you're onto territory that will give you a massive insight into the 'hidden' self. It also helps if one of your planets is in the same sign as your Aquarian's as it gives you a comfortable 'I recognise' you type of feeling.

My Mum and I have the same Moon signs so on some levels we get on, but because my Moon (Gemini)is square my own Sun-sign (Pisces) the whole subject of nurturing and being nice to my inner self is more of a task.

The Moon is also our 'inner child'. The part of us that is young and playful, needy and in need of, soft and sensitive mothering . However, if your Moon is in the sign of Capricorn you have to somehow incorporate the very grown up word 'realistic' into the mix.

This is the wonder of Astrology. The language of it! Because it isn't just the planets in the sky, it's the way we write about them or talk about them or on a deeper level, experience them. When I look at a birth chart I have to take all the little bits here and there, consolidate them all, make sense of them, then translate it all so my clients can understand, in simple English, what it all means.

It's pointless you knowing that your Moon is in the sign of Scorpio if you don't know what it means...and with that meaning comes a bit of (self) understanding and hopefully some ability to feel at peace with yourself. In a chart, some things are more important than others. They sort of shout at you and go 'look at me, I need understanding' while other things just merge into the background.

Astrology isn't static, it evolves with each new generation that experiences it. Yes, it's based on something ancient but it's perfectly applicable in this 'modern age'. It always will be because Astrology is another way of making sense of our world.

So when I say that the Moon in Astrology covers our emotional needs, what I'm saying is once you give some consideration to the type of Moon you have, you can experiment with allowing it a bit of slack.

I wouldn't expect someone with Moon in Capricorn to enjoy being the youngest or most inexperienced in a group of people. They would feel better being older, in charge, looked-up to, respected, the voice of authority......

In our example chart, Oprah Winfrey has her Moon in the sign of Sagittarius. This means she has strong beliefs (that she doesn't like challenged) and because it is in a Fire sign it means her emotional expression is fast and active.

## The Dr Bach Flower Essences

In 1933 Dr Edward Bach a medical doctor and Homeopath

published a little booklet called 'The Twelve Healers and other remedies'. His theory was that if the emotional disturbance a person was suffering from was removed, their illness would also disappear. I tend to agree with this kind of thinking as most illnesses (except being hit by a bus) are preceded by an unhappy event or an emotional disruption that then sets into place the body getting out of sync. Removing the emotional issue and bringing a bit of stablity into someone's life, when they are having a hard time, can improve their overall health so much that wellness resumes.

Knowing which Bach Flower Essence can help certain worries and gives you and your Aquarius more control over your lives. I recommend the essences a lot in my practice if I feel a certain part of a person's chart is under stress...and usually it's the Moon that needs help.

The essences describe the negative aspects of the character, which are focused on during treatment. This awareness helps reverse those trends, so when our emotional selves are nice and comfortable, we can then face each day with more strength.

I've quoted Dr Bach's actual words for each sign.

To use the Essences take 2 drops from the stock bottle and put it into a glass of water and sip. I tend to recommend putting them into a small water bottle, and sipping them through-out the day, at least 4 times. For young children, do the same.

*Remember to seek medical attention if symptoms don't get better and/or seek professional counselling.*

## Aries Moon

*"Blame it or praise it, there is no denying the wild horse in us."*
Virginia Woolf

Aries is a Fire Sign and as such makes an Aquarius native very confident- it can also incline them to being bossy and opinionated. They will react very quickly to things especially on the emotional level. They will blow-up quickly and just as rapidly cool down and wonder what all the fuss was. On the positive side they won't harbour a grudge and are super people for getting projects off the ground.

*Bach Flower Essence Impatiens:*

*'Those who are quick in thought and action and who wish all things to be done without hesitation or delay.'*

## Taurus Moon

*"If you want to eat well in England, eat three breakfasts."...*

*"Money is like a sixth sense without which you cannot make a complete use of the other five."*

W. Somerset Maugham

Taurus is an Earth sign, concerned with things it can touch, taste and enjoy. This Aquarius will worry about and focus on food and money. They like luxury and the 'best' of everything. They can be inclined to indulge in exotic chocolate or wine and then worry about paying the bills. They need stability, routine and emotionally are slow to react. As Taurus is an Earth sign things associated with an earthy nature come into play so their physical/sexual needs will be important. They will hold onto things for years and can find it hard to throw stuff away. Learning how to 'let go' is a useful lesson otherwise the loft, the garage and lots of boxes get filled with things they equate with memories or good feelings.

*Bach Flower Essence Gentian :*

*'Those who are easily discouraged. They may be progressing well in the affairs of their daily life, but any small delay or hindrance to progress causes doubt and soon disheartens them"*

## Gemini Moon

*"Sometimes the biggest problem is in your head. You've got to believe you can play a shot instead of wondering where your next bad shot is coming from."*

Jack Nicklaus

Gemini is an Air sign and delights in thoughts, ideas and conversation. Here your Aquarius will have a need to chat and have opinions acknowledged, discussed, thought about, talked over, and contemplated. Brothers and sisters are important so are short journeys. If you want to get a Moon in Gemini to spill the beans about how they feel about something, pop them in a car and take them for a short journey, then ask your question and they will quite happily tell you things they might never say face-to-face. Oh, and they love books and reading because they 'keep the mind active'.

*Bach Flower Essence Cerato:*

*'Those who have not sufficient confidence in themselves to make their own decisions'*

This Essence comes under the heading 'For Those Who Suffer Uncertainty' (which Libra and Gemini both suffer from.)

## Cancer Moon

*"I love the physical thing of being on the earth that bore you."*

Jacqueline du Pre

Nurturing is important. Wanting to hold things close and never let them go. Food, family and home are all important. As a Water sign Moon they feel things very acutely and will sulk if you don't acknowledge how they feel. They love home-cooking, pets, snugly clothes and on a bad day can worry about money and 'is-there-enough-to-go-around?' When I do readings for clients with Moon in Cancer, they're always quite happy for me to make charts for the whole of their family, their children/partner/parents/siblings and I almost have to drag them back to talking about and focussing on themselves.

*Bach Flower Essence Clematis:*

*'Living in the hopes of happier times, when their ideals may come true.'*

## Leo Moon

*"Leo lends a nobility to the emotions, but his placement also makes it difficult to back down or to compromise."*

Joan McEvers

As another Fire sign, Leo Moon says: 'Please recognise me, know my name, smile at me, treat me with respect and roll out the red carpet. Be my friend, be my exclusive friend.' My mother had an Aquarius friend who had Moon in Leo and she was perfectly happy to see my (now) elderly mother every weekend, take her out for a short drive to a garden centre or a charity shop and play Lexicon together. She had a receptive audience in my Mum (Moon in Gemini) and the two of them enjoyed the regular contact (Aquarius is a fixed sign). This lovely lady had a captive audience in my Mum, something she really enjoyed and someone to play the keyboards to and sing to....wonderful.

*Bach Flower Essence Vervain:*

*'Those with fixed principles and ideas, which they are confident are right'*

## Virgo Moon

*"I just do all the things one would do for any human being to try to make them feel better. You don't mind if I smoke?"*

Vanessa Redgrave

Worry, worry and more worry about health, symptoms, what I ate, will I live long enough to follow my dream/path in life? Virgo is an Earth sign but is also what we call a Mutable sign, given to change and living in the past. It's quite a tricky Moon for an Aquarius to have because on the one hand they want to heal and be healed and on the other they want independence and their own ideas and space. An Aquarius with this Moon will remember teeny little details which if you've got Sagittarius planets, will seem remarkable and irrelevant. Keeping calm is a helpful attribute so make sure you have strategies to help them with this.

*Bach Flower Essence Centuary:*

*'Their good nature leads them to do more than their own share of work and they may neglect their own mission in life.'*

## Libra Moon

*"I feel I need to understand my relationships better, why I don't manage to choose easy people or situations to be in. I like a challenge but crave stability (which I'd probably dislike)."*

Client E, female

Another Air sign, full of ideas. Be fair, surround them with pastel shades and don't argue with them (unless they start the argument!). Libra is ruled by Venus the Goddess of Love, so pleasing, gentle, fair and 'nice' things will always go down well. As with all Libra planets they feel far better in a relationship, than out of one but as an Aquarius those relationships might be quite diverse. The also suffer from terrible indecision. Should I do this, or would it be best to do that…or will I upset so and so if I do the other? They will tie themselves in knots 'trying' to find the best solution to something.

*Bach Flower Essence Scleranthus:*

*'Those who suffer from being unable to decide between two things, first one seeming right then the other.'*

## Scorpio Moon

*"Yeah, I think that it's important once you get on national*

*television you make sure your fly is up, 'course you don't want anything unnecessary happening - like exposure."*
Robbie Williams

Another Water sign but this one is so intense. Don't ask too many questions, don't pry, they need to trust you first. On the positive side they can get to the centre of a problem and on the negative suffer paranoia: 'Everyone is against me' syndrome. There's no grey with them. It's a case of black and white. If you want someone to run your secret society, here's your man/woman.

*Bach Flower Essence Chicory*:
'They are continually correcting what they consider wrong and enjoy doing so.'

## Sagittarius Moon
*"Turn your wounds into wisdom."*
Oprah Winfrey

Another Fire sign. Let's go to Machu Picchu in Peru! Let's find the meaning of life, let's study some weird way-out religion. Let's also drop our foot in it and say things that leave you gasping for air! You're fat! This lettuce is terrible! You've got a hole in your shirt! The don't want to hurt your feelings but they just can't resist pointing out the b****** obvious because their emotions are tuned into, what for them is 'the truth'. And it can work both ways. Some people like their 'honesty', other cringe about their lack of sensitivity. Both Oprah Winfrey and Yoko Ono are Aquarians with Moon in Sag, but Oprah is respected while Yoko had to struggle to be 'seen' separately from the glow from John Lennon.

*Bach Flower Essence Agrimony*:
This Essence comes under the heading 'Over-Sensitive to Influences and Ideas'
*'They hide their cares behind their humor and jesting and try to bear*

*their trials with cheerfulness.'*

## Capricorn Moon

*"A scientific man ought to have no wishes, no affections, - a mere heart of stone."*
Charles Darwin

An Earth sign and a very serious Moon. Capricorn Moon reads the Guardian or listens to serious plays, classical music, crazy comedies and wants the reality of life not the fluff. This sign combination doesn't do fluff very well. They like ancient things, prefer older friends and acquaintances and often feel happier in a studious or serious environment. So many older famous Aquarians such as Abraham Lincoln and Charles Darwin had this combination and could withstand opposition and emotional severity that would make modern day humans crumble and they certainly won't share any of their fears or weaknesses with you. Think of the word 'stoic'.

*Bach Fower Essence Mimulus:*
*'Fear of wordly things, illness, pain, accident, poverty, of dark, of being alone, of misfortune. They secretly bear their dread and do not speak freely of it to others'*

## Aquarius Moon

*"Remember: Always walk in the light. And if you feel like you're not walking in it, go find it. Love the light."*
Roberta Flack

Another Air sign. This makes a Double Aquarius. They are strange, weird wonderful and different and that's without even trying. Underneath all that wackiness can sometimes be a little sadness as they can have had a rather severe upbringing. I have found that clients with Moon in Aquarius have had to stifle their emotions when little, so when they grow up, they don't express them easily. They can certainly manage on their own. I know one Aquarius who lives an almost a monastic existence and he is perfectly happy with that. He likes company but doesn't want to marry or have kids. A total outsider. Living on the fringes of life...and he doesn't have a mobile phone...

*Bach Flower Essence Water Violet:*

*'For those who like to be alone, very independent, capable and self-reliant. They are aloof and go their own way.'*

## Pisces Moon

*"You only grow when you are alone."*

Paul Newman

This is *the* most sensitive Moon sign for anyone to have and it can suffer unnecessarily by ignoring that sensitivity. They can be psychic, caring, muddled, sensitive, touchy, dreamy and more muddled the more they are made to do things that are brash, noisy or violent. My clients with this combination need space to express their inner-most fears, which are many and are at odds with their Aquarius quirky Sun. If they allow that sensitivity some space, they feel a whole lot better.

*Bach Fower Essence Rock Rose:*

*'For cases where there even appears no hope or when the person is very frightened or terrified.'*

*Chapter Five*

# The Houses

In Astrology the Sun is how we shine and the houses are where we shine. Having your Sun in the 5<sup>th</sup> house of creativity and play, is radically different from having it in the 12<sup>th</sup> house of spirituality and self sacrifice.

To understand your Aquarius friend or relative fully, it's good to know what house their Sun is in so you can understand what sort of Aquarius they are and what motivates them.

It's also the most complicated concept for people to get their heads around. What is a house? What does it mean to have a planet in a house?

If you imagine the houses are like little rooms, each one further down a corridor. If the Sun (who the person is) is in the first house, in the first room in the corridor, then everyone at the beginning of the corridor can hear that person when they talk, can probably hear them when they cough and can certainly hear them if they shout. Now if their Sun (who they are) is in a room further down the corridor, say in the 6<sup>th</sup> house, it won't be so easy to hear or judge what's happening to them in their little room....so you have to go along the corridor to meet them and make contact. And when their Sun is in the 12<sup>th</sup> house, in the last room in the corridor, then you might never meet them. They might happily exist without you ever going that far down the corridor to find them. They won't come and find you but after a time, you might end up near to where they are, that's if you hang around in the corridor for long enough .

People with their Sun in the 12<sup>th</sup> house don't want to be in the limelight, whilst people with their Sun in the 1<sup>st</sup> house (right at the beginning of the corridor) enjoy the fact that people know who they are and where they are.

Oprah has her Sun in the 2<sup>nd</sup> house, so financial security is important to her, which it would have to be because she is worth over $ 2.7 billion! It's not just the money that's important to her though, it's what the money will bring for her: "What material success does is provide you with the ability to concentrate on other things that really matter. And that is being able to make a difference, not only in your own life, but in other people's lives."

I have included underneath, which Ascendant will come with the Sun being in each house, as using the Equal House System means all the houses are the same size, but the Ascendants can be one or other of two signs depending on the time of birth.

## The First House, House of Personality

*"Newman's first law: It is useless to put on your brakes when you're upside down."*
Paul Newman

The first house is all about the 'self' so an Aquarius with 1<sup>st</sup> house Sun will be quite focused on that, themselves. They are generally confident, self-assured, positive and fearless. Ruled by Mars the God of War they will want to get on with things, be upbeat and action orientated.

(Ascendant Aquarius or Capricorn).

## The Second House, House of Money, Material Possessions and Self-Worth

*"I am in charge of all the finances at home and like to keep it this way. I like the idea and reality of having a secret nest egg hidden away in case my family should ever need it."*
Melissa Corkhill

The second house is concerned with the material world: money,

possessions, food, sensuality as it is ruled by Venus the Goddess of Love. An Aquarius with Sun here will need to have a secure home, a solid income and money for a 'rainy-day' to feel truly happy.
(Ascendant Capricorn or Sagittarius).

### The Third House, House of Communication & Short Journeys
*"A man's friendships are one of the best measures of his worth."*
Charles Darwin

The third house covers siblings, short journeys and all forms of communication and the Aquarius Sun here will favour these levels of being. They might be chatty, enjoy talking, teaching, making a quick little trip to the shops, or a short walk to a neighbours. Ruled by Mercury the messenger God, they will make sure the mobile is turned on and in credit.
(Ascendant Sagittarius or Scorpio)

### The Fourth House, House of Home, Family & Roots
*"I would like to marry and have more children. I would like to try and do it right."*
Phil Collins

The home life and domestic concerns are the essence of the fourth house. Mum, relatives, dinner, family and food. Concerns will be centred on relations and things close to home. An Aquarius with their Sun here will be less of a 'typical' Aquarius as their domestic life will make them seem 'cosy'. Pop stars don't survive well with this placement. Clients of mine are more shy and home-loving than other Aquarians. In fact if you want a nice childhood, rejoice if your parent/s own this placement!
(Ascendant Scorpio or Libra)

## The Fifth House, House of Creativity & Romance

*"And I want my writing to grow and be a white haired child forever playing in the garden"*
novelist Lucy English

Sun in the fifth house is similar to having a Leo Ascendant. Notice me. Don't ignore me, be my friend. Children are important as are having as many 'followers' as possible. As this is the house of creativity, this could manifest as babies, Art, music, and/or poetry. They love to create and even more love you to appreciate and acknowledge what they create.

(Ascendant Libra or Virgo)

## The Sixth House, House of Work & Health

*"Ask the right questions if you're to find the right answers."*
Vanessa Redgrave

Health, welfare, healing all tune into the sixth house association and links with Virgo, the 6th sign of the zodiac. So you have concern for their wellbeing  and the need to work in an orderly manner. A place for everything and everything in its place. Doesn't mean they can't be untidy but does mean they will have categorised every thought and every feeling into neat little compartments.

(Ascendant Virgo or Leo)

## The Seventh House, House of Relationships & Marriage

*"I just wanted to capture the feeling you get on a summer day when you're drunk and you're rolling about on the grass with the person you love next to you."*
Robbie Williams

Partnerships, lovers and marriage are starred in the seventh house. Anxiety about husbands and wives not to mention the whole gamut of problems with or in matrimony. I personally know both variations and the Leo Ascendant will want the red-carpet treatment as well as the comfort and security of marriage, even if it means marrying more than once.

(Ascendant Leo or Cancer)

## The Eighth House, House of Life Force in Birth, Sex, Death & After-Life

*"Every secret of a writer's soul, every experience of his life, every quality of his mind is written large in his works."*
Virginia Woolf

Sex, death, reincarnation and 'deep meaningful things'. Maybe even a slight inclination towards obsession and intensity. Eighth house Sun's are happiest solving some complex, secret problem. Jobs might be investigator, spy or researcher. If they have a Gemini Ascendant then there is a horrible dilemma of on the one hand wanting all this secrecy, and on the other of wanting to tell all to everyone.

(Ascendant Cancer or Gemini)

## The Ninth House, House of Philosophy & Long Distance Travel

*"The house was in a Portuguese neighbourhood and near the Catholic church, which I loved to peep into and see the candles burning in the cool white pillared interior."*
Jean English (A Vanished World, My Memories)

Religion and philosophy are covered by this house. The ninth house governs long distance travel, as opposed to the third house which governs short journeys, so natives love other countries, journeys to distant lands, further education and learning.

My Mum converted to Catholicism, having spent 10 early

years living in Hong Kong, then she lived in Ceylon (Sri Lanka) after marriage and later Switzerland when my Dad was promoted.

(Ascendant Gemini or Taurus)

## The Tenth House, House of Social Identity & Career

*"In chamber music, companionship and hard work are combined as long as the other players don't feel lazy."*
Jacqueline du Pre

The tenth house is all about career. People with their Sun sign in this house want to make a mark in the world and rise above earthly constraints. When I see them in private practice, they are mostly concerned with their 'path in life' and wanting to be seen to be doing good and having high social standing. There can be a concern about 'what others think of me'.

(Ascendant Taurus or Aries)

## The Eleventh House, House of Social Life & Friendships

*"And that's what makes this a great game, is the support and the commitment that the fans give the game."*
Nolan Ryan

This is the 'true' house for an Aquarius as they are the 11th sign of the Zodiac and the eleventh house has a similar meaning. Natives will want, no *need*: friends, groups, organisations affiliations, societies that they can/will be members of. They don't see themselves in isolation to the world, they are part of it.

(Ascendant Aries or Pisces)

## The Twelfth House, House of Spirituality

*"Developing the muscles of the soul demands no competitive spirit, no killer instinct, although it may erect pain barriers that the spiritual athlete must crash through."*

Germaine Greer

I have noticed a lot of my clients who have Sun in the twelfth, really don't like living in the lime-light. They want to be in the background, working behind the scenes. If you want someone to support you or your project, carefully holding you and content to stay un-noticed, then choose someone with Sun in the 12th. However, you're also very unlikely to meet too many of these private people as, un-like other Aquarians, they're not dreadfully sociable.

(Ascendant Pisces or Aquarius)

*Chapter Six*

# The Difficulties

Every sign of the Zodiac has a 'difficult' side. People complain that Scorpios are secretive and sexed-up, that Geminis can't keep a secret, and Sagittarians always put their foot in their mouth. Aquarians are no different. There are people who will complain about any star sign, when they feel that they are being misunderstood. In writing this book I had to consider what were the most common complaints thrown at Aquarians, and as this is a practical book, how to address those complaints and find easy-to-use solutions.

### Gemini female talking about Aquarians in her family

*"My Dad and youngest sister are Aquarians, I find them both opinionated and dominant. They feel they are always right and no one should dare to challenge them! Perhaps it's because they are related. They also are very witty, very humourous people, both very insecure, hate being alone both living abroad, both heavy drinkers. Not good at seeing their own faults but critical and intolerant of others!"*

But first we will cover the difficulties. And as always, we have to consider what sign and Element *you* are to be able to offer the best advice. I would never suggest to a Cancer that their feelings are unimportant. That would be like asking them to chop off their hands or jump off a cliff. It's not do-able or helpful. I have also collected the most common complaints people have about Aquarians, taking into account that if things were going well for the person, those difficulties would not arise. As I mentioned earlier, you are less likely to have a complaint about an Aquarius than a Pisces as Aquarians have a more inclusive type of energy and maybe one that is easier to define.

So, what are the major problems?

## My Aquarius is so cool, I feel I'm living in the Antartic.

This is I'm afraid the biggest complaint I hear in practice about Aquarians. It comes in various different disguises. It's not that your Aquarius wants to make you feel isolated and alone. They also certainly don't want you to feel neglected but your average Aquarius isn't huggy-touchy-feely and will also allow you (what they like themselves) LOTS OF SPACE.

Now some star signs find the space thing very distressing. They like to snuggle-up to people and physically feel their presence. They are kinaesthetic and want to touch you as they talk to you, connect with your body (as well as your mind) ....now these are things that will send your Aquarius running for the door. Snuggle up?? Touch?? However, they might just manage this with a pet but with a human it's rather harder for them. So try not to get distressed about it and get your physical needs met by massage from a good therapist or owning a pet who will enjoy being petted.

## My Aquarius says they don't love me anymore but they want us to stay friends.

Ah ha. Now we're getting into something that a lot of women don't understand. An Aquarius man (or woman) is being polite here. If your Aquarius doesn't love you, then you need to walk away from any ideas of romance. However, they will still want to 'stay friends'. Why? How? You may ask. It's a difficult state. I know so many Aquarians who stay friends with ex-partners and their new partner just can't understand how they can want to go for long walks, chat, share lunch, have a laugh with someone they're not dating....it gets certain signs really jealous....But they're not understanding how an Aquarius works. They don't want to lose your friendship and that is THE most important part of knowing someone to them. And remember they are also a 'fixed sign'. The fixed signs are Taurus, Scorpio and Aquarius, and they don't like change. To lose contact with you altogether is a big change they'd rather not make.

## My Aquarius has got into a routine and says he/she is bored.

Oh dear. This is one that should be ringing alarm bells. A bored Aquarius is an Aquarius whose life is hanging on a thread. Why has your Aquarius got bored? Have you been preventing them from creative thinking? Are you an Earth or Water sign? If you want to stay in your Aquarian's world, you better resolve this one swiftly and promptly. Don't worry about the finer details of the problem, get moving.

Encourage your Aquarius to join a group. Any group. It could be pottery or Art classes, or making paper animals, or poetry. It could be kayaking in a lake in Seattle or pot-holing in Blackburn or cycling in Japan. Anything as long as there are other people doing something. This is better than them moping around at home driving you insane. Lend them money to get a hair-cut. Sell your car and buy a new one and drive them round in it for a few hours. At the very least ask your Aquarius to record their dreams for the next six nights and help them unravel what is preventing them from getting out of that (horrible for them) routine.

## My Aquarius wants to go by bicycle to Moldava and study wine-making for the next 6 months so they can come home and create their own vineyard in Clacton-on-sea.

Rest assured that if your Aquarius wants to do this, nothing you say or do will stop them short of locking them up in the bedroom, which I really don't recommend. First of all your Aquarius has 'got an idea', secondly Aquarius ideas are the life and blood of their lives and stopping them from living out those ideas is the quickest way to push them away from you.

The unhappiest Aquarians I meet in private practice have run out of ideas. This generally happens if they live with Water signs, as the Water signs (tend to) pour cold water all over their ideas because they want their Aquarius to nurture their feelings....and you can't do that if you're hundreds of miles away. Or they're living with Earth signs who just can't keep up with the barrage of original thought and will ask questions like: " How will your bike get to Moldava, it can't even get into town without something falling off."...or "You don't even *like* drinking wine, how are your going to start a vineyard?" and so on.

The Earth signs, unfortunately don't 'do' things without planning them carefully first, checking the legitimacy of the concept and generally only 'do' things that have-been-done-before.

I tend to think that creative thinking was what brought about hundreds of inventions and the breaking of new records from things like flying to computers. So, if this is your Aquarius, get them a mobile phone, check they have got a good map....and wave them goodbye. Meanwhile you can either join them, or make the beds ready for when they come home.

### My Aquarius has so many friends I can't keep track.

Personally, I've never had a problem with this issue. It's sort of part and parcel with living with an Aquarius. With so many in my house-hold as I was growing up, I thought everybody had that amount of friends. It wasn't until I re-married that I discovered people that don't have friends and their family is who they 'socialise' with. If you're an Air sign this won't be too much of a problem as you'll probably enjoy all the extra company. The same applies if you're a Fire sign. As long as a Fire sign has an audience, which Aquarians can provide easily, they're happy.

The difficulties arise if you're an Earth sign as that amount of people running through your life will exhaust you.

## How do I deal with my Aquarius living on their own planet and in their own head space?

Now this really is a difficulty for all the Earth signs out there and was proposed by a lovely Taurean lady I know. Her Aquarius isn't demonstrative enough. She loves his sense of freedom, his original ideas, his quirkiness but after having a number of children and 'making house' with him, she then got all upset about getting older and not being sexy anymore. She wanted to be wined and dined and made a fuss of. She wanted to return to the excitement of their earlier lives and as a Taurus was feeling stuck, and that stuckness (which Taurus equates with stability) was driving her crazy. She didn't want to leave him, she didn't want to hurt his feelings too much but her own sense of needing to find she was still attractive in her 40's was driving her (and him) to distraction.

She felt he was too far away from her. That he wasn't 'there' for her. Interestingly enough, they both have Sun in the 6th house, so they were both worried about the situation and luckily enough both had the presence of mind to be able to talk about it. To deal with an Aquarius 'on their own planet' you need to take into account your own needs and how to fulfil them, because your Aquarius will give you what they want...which is tons of freedom. In fact she also complained that he gave her too *much* freedom! For a Taurus to feel happy with an Aquarius they need to state clearly and succinctly what they need in the relationship.

They need their Aquarius to 'be' in their physical world. To acknowledge their existence. Comment on their clothes or their hair or the food they cook. To cuddle them when they're feeling down, stroke them gently and contact their bodies....not their minds. This might not happen in this particular relationship, so my advice would be to get those needs met somewhere else.

Have a regular massage with someone who enjoys giving the massage. Nothing sexual, just something where the body is feeling touched and embraced. Maybe become a Life Model in an Art Class where the body would be subject of attention and consideration.

*Chapter Seven*

# The Solutions

Ok, you now know how to make a chart, where the Sun is located, what sign the Moon is in...and everything is hunky-dory...

No?

Well. In everyone's life you can come across difficulties and upsetments. There you are, nicely bonded/bonding with your Aquarian when suddenly your life falls apart. What you thought was true love, understanding or delight has now turned to sorrow, unhappiness or confusion.

Don't fret. There are solutions to every problem, the trick is to get an understanding of the person suffering from the problem and help them feel better. You can easily do that and in helping them feeling better, you will feel better too.

This is of course assuming that you are close enough to the Aquarian in your life to make a difference. If miles separate you, my advice might need a bit of adjustment, but don't be deterred.

Death might also separate you from the person you are trying to have a relationship with. A parent might die, a child might have been snatched away from you, a relative or friend might no longer be on the earthly plane. Don't despair, you can just as easily contact someone 'in spirit' as you can on earth, you just need to adapt things to suit.

Now you need two things in your toolbox of solutions:

Access to the internet and the wonderful website www.emofree.com

The Bach Flower Essences mentioned earlier for each Moon sign.

I will now give you an example of the sort of things that upset Aquarians.

This lady emailed me because she believes she is an adult indigo.

*"Hello Mary,*

*I saw your name on the Indigo Network. I'm probably an adult indigo, born \* Jan 19\*\* one month ahead of due date. People tell me I look about 15 years younger than I am and I have occasionally had children not recognize that I am an adult. I don't really feel like one. I've always been extremely sensitive and empathetic, and had difficulty communicating with people effectively and issues with authority. Most of all a sense of nobody wanting to play my game (where everyone loves and cooperates with each other and there is no judgement, criticism, taking, backstabbing). It's just that most people are a whole different species from me. I've been through the most challenging experiences over the last 15 years or so since starting on a spiritual path, but just lately am starting to see a reason for it. I have also become increasingly aware of my longing to find communities of other people who are on the same wavelength, as well as the fear that I am not following my vocation to change the world.*

*Hope to hear from you..."*

Now this lady has Virgo Ascendant, Sun in the 5<sup>th</sup> house and a Scorpio Moon.

To offer her advice we'd need to take into account the following things. As she has a Virgo Ascendant, we know she's going to worry (all Virgos are worriers), so first off, we need to offer her advice on how to reduce the worry.

The flower essences help here, as does the emotional freedom technique.

We would then need to make some suggestions about needing to find something to do to help her feel creative, as she has Moon in the 5<sup>th</sup> house, and the 5<sup>th</sup> house covers creativity. I don't know if she can change the world, but she certainly can change her own world by taking up a hobby or being creative or artistic. Virgo Ascendant does give her an interest in healing, as Virgo covers health, so maybe a good course in a healing discipline would help her find her path. Needing to find a 'community' of like-minded people is a constant desire for almost all Aquarians, and places like the Findhorn Foundation in Scotland certainly fit the bill.

Then not forgetting the Scorpio Moon, we must be sure that she feels safe and secure and not threatened by others, as in the past she's had problems with 'backstabbing'. All in all being self-employed would probably fit the bill and also doing some sort of charitable work.

Here are some suggestions for the Aquarius in your life, how to help and what to do when things get difficult.

## Aries Ascendant or Moon

If your Aquarius is upset you're going to have to be quick here, because this sign combination moves fast. Here they will need some action. Aries is ruled by the planet Mars so the best solution for an upset Aquarius with an Ascendant in such a strong sign is to get them out of the house, for a long walk. Talking about this won't wash. The Aries Ascendant will want ACTION (as opposed to Leo who wants LIGHTS! CAMERA! ACTION!). A Tai-chi class, Judo, running, fencing, action-based sports. Not competitive as this combination is likely to bop you on the head if they don't get their way, and this book is written to help the Aquarian friend......

## Taurus Ascendant or Moon

Now this person's energies are slower. To make your Aquarian feel better get some cakes (low fat, sugar free) out of the cupboard. Listen for a few minutes, then get them booked-in for a holistic, healing, aromatherapy massage. Sooner rather than later. Taurus wants their basic needs met and those needs are for food, sex, and touch . The BODY is important here.

### Gemini Ascendant or Moon

Get the kettle on. Get the books out. Discuss. Discuss some more. Look at workable solutions. Listen. Nod your head every now and then. Smile. Look confident and speak as if you know how they are feeling/thinking. Take them for a short, local drive in the car and they'll soon spill the beans. Get them talking as the cerebral, air energies need to think and they can't think if they're upset, but talking about what's going on will help them focus their thinking.

### Cancer Ascendant or Moon

Oodles of sympathy is needed here. Cancer is a Water sign, and in contrast to the Aquarius Sun, makes a person who really needs EMPATHY. You can't just cluck and look interested here. Unless you have suffered what Cancer has, you're out of the game. Best strategy is to put the kettle on, turn off your mobile, look calm and sympathetic, lean into the Cancer's space, mirror their body language, and get the tissues handy. Cancerians need to cry and will generally feel much better afterwards.

### Leo Ascendant or Moon

The Second Fire sign of the Zodiac. You'd never guess it though because Leo thinks they  are special and unique and they need lots and lots of attention. 'There, there, there,' works well. So does "How can I help, what can I DO?" The Fire signs like action, Aries likes physical action, while Leo likes company action. They want an audience to demonstrate and act out their story to. The more the merrier! You won't need tissues. Leo has to be really suffering to cry and they tend to do so in the quiet and alone.

## Virgo Ascendant or Moon

I was tempted to say get the doctor round as Virgo is so concerned with their health. When they're upset, a Virgo/Aquarius will fret, and fret and fret, until you feel like screaming "CALM DOWN". This isn't a helpful strategy but it does come to mind when you've heard every little detail of whatever was happening. But I'm not going to criticise Virgo, because they have that beautiful capacity to heal that no other star sign has. If only they'd see that in themself, and instead of fretting about their own health, they could be busy healing themselves or others. Virgo/Aquarius won't really want to talk, as talking makes them feel worse. They will feel better if they take a flower essence. Centaury is good or the Homeopathic remedy Ignatia, for hysteria, grief and upset. Emotional upsets will also affect a Virgo/Aquarius' physical health so if they're under stress they'll get tummy troubles, or asthma or a whole host of seemingly unrelated health conditions, when what they really need to do is lie down in the quiet and turn their brains off for a while.

## Libra Ascendant or Moon

You will need calm and tranquil pleasant surroundings – white lilies will be very pleasing to their aesthetic senses. Libra/Aquarius is very sensitive to their environment and as Libra is ruled by Venus, they respond better to beauty, harmony and no discord. They might need gentle promoting to start talking about it, a beautiful tea tray with a jasmine tissane is good. Even better would be a bunch of roses or a gentle aromatherapy massage. Things need to be balanced for Libra/Aquarius and they need to feel that everything is fair. They will want to consider everyone else's point of view, but it can lead to indecision that will only tire them even more, so it would be best to find just one strategy to move forward with.

## Scorpio Ascendant or Moon

Not much is going to be visible with this combination. They feel things so deeply and intensely that if you were capable of seeing what they were feeling, you'd be shocked. Dark colours, blood red, deep yearnings. The solution is to allow them plenty of space. Somewhere where they can brood and ponder and yearn without it sucking in everything in their orbit like a black-hole. In fact if you imagine black-holes you won't be far off what this combination is all about. If you're a strong person, stand within reach and be centered. If you're a bit fluffy, go shopping until they have recovered. There is not much you can do to help as they will prefer to lose themselves in the emotion. They might write a song or a poem, get horribly drunk, or take large amounts of drugs. They might want revenge so be watchful of this and be aware that if there are other people involved when a Scorpio/Aquarius is worked-up, heads might roll. One useful tip is to get your Scorpio/Aquarius to write a letter addressed to the people concerned, then ritualistically burn it. Doing radical things like this will help considerably.

## Sagittarius Ascendant or Moon

If you can visit a church or spiritual retreat, or you know a Tibetan monk, it will help things considerably. The Sagittarius aspect of this combination needs to understand the spiritual whys and wherefores. Anything by a divine adept will make a Sagittarius/Aquarian give some meaning to their circumstances. Oh, and they might make some very blunt or personal remarks, just ignore them!

## Capricorn Ascendant or Moon

Be practical, realistic and get the dry sense of humour dusted off. This combination respond well to old fashioned good manners and good humour – watch a black-and-white classic movie together before you discuss the serious stuff. First get everything that has gone wrong into some sort of sensible perspective. Talk about the real things, the money, the plans, the future. Once they have a clear future-based goal, they will cheer up enormously.You will have to discuss the truth and not hide behind niceties. Aquarius-Libra combinations are happy for everyone to get on, Aquarius-Capricorn combinations will prefer one solution, one winner, one loser. They'd (obviously) prefer not to be the loser, but generally in life, they don't expect too much, so are rarely disappointed. They just expect everything to get worse. Try and guide them towards the idea that it is OK to have fun and enjoy life.....

## Aquarius Ascendant or Moon

Any major charity being mentioned will always help as Aquarius is the sign of autonomy and things that benefit mankind. I once recommended to a client who had someone with a Moon in Aquarius in his life, to give money to her favourite charity, as that would help her understand how devoted he was to her. If you can bring the wider-world into the equation, so much the better. Make sure their sense of freedom and individuality hasn't been removed and correct any signs that it may have, as otherwise you'll have a total breakdown on your hands.

## Pisces Ascendant or Moon

This is the sign combination of sensitivity. Please be gentle with them. Imagine they are beings with gossamer wings, angels in disguise, beings from another planet, and you'll have more of an idea of how to help them. They won't really listen to what you tell them, they'll sense it, but you might feel that nothing sank in. It did. It will just take a while to filter through all the other stuff that is in their heads. Light a candle, burn incense, lay out some Angel Cards or use some other form of divination to help you. The I-Ching is good and I know Aquarians with this combination who will believe the oracle more than a letter from the bank or a discussion with a trusted friend. So learn a little psychic technique or two and use them to assist you both.

*Chapter Eight*

# Bonding Tactics

*"Bonding with an Aquarian is that you can't make it happen. Loyalty is important to us and our often random mind can be challenging to follow. I wonder if we often seem much deeper than we actually are - take us at face value and stick with us for a while and let the bonding happen slowly."*
Female Aquarius

### Strategies to help you bond with an Aquarius

I suppose the question that needs to be asked is why do you want to bond with this particular Aquarius? If it's for love you'd better make sure you have left enough room for them to do their own thing.

One of the longest running marriages in Hollywood was Paul Newman and Joanne Woodwood. She has Sun in Pisces, Moon in Aquarius and he had Sun in Aquarius, Moon in Pisces. Just those two factors alone kept them together for over 50 years until his death in 2009.

Interviewed by Hello magazine Joanne Woodward described being married to Paul as: *"Being married to the most considerate, romantic man."* He said: *"We are very, very different people and yet somehow we feed off those varied differences, and instead of separating us, it has made the whole bond a lot stronger."*

So here we have the key to their relationship lasting so well, Joanne allowed him to be/do whatever made him happy, and he in turn was considerate and romantic. What more would a girl want?

Move on forwards by 30 years to the birth of Paris Hilton (Sun in Aquarius, Moon in Leo, Sagittarius Ascendant) and here we have someone who has made herself famous for her rebellious attitude. Last seen dating Doug Reinhardt, a Libran with Moon in Aquarius, another nice little Sun/Moon connection.

Unless you are prepared to offer freedom and space to an Aquarius, don't waste your time trying to get to know them, let alone dating them.

My mother dated a number of men before she finally settled down and noted in her memoirs, 'A Vanished World': "*I don't really know what made me break off the engagement...I handed back the ring without any proper explanation...what a relief it was to have escaped the noose.*" Which sort of sums-up an Aquarius thinking about a) the loss of freedom and b) there was no hurry to find 'Mr Right'.

Also, as I have emphasized in my first book How To Survive a Pisces, remember what sign *you* are. It's no good dating an Aquarius if you're a Cancer, then complaining that they are 'cold' or 'not emotional'. That's a bit like buying an ice-cream then complaining it's cold. It's supposed to be cold.

"*I dislike when people accuse Aquarians of not being emotional - I often feel emotive and I am reasonably good at empathising.*"

However, you have to decide what emotions are for you, then work on from there. An Aquarian's emotions are cerebral, based on the areas we have discussed (freedom, differentness) and while they will be emotional about those areas, they are more likely to adjust to life's problems regarding dating in a matter-of-fact manner. It also really depends on what other planets they have in their chart, as an Aquarius with lots of Pisces planets is going to tackle life in a far more Piscean way, than Aquarius.

I must stress, though, that the whole subject of dating and marrying is less of a feature for Aquarians. They know what they want, they know what they like, and they are much less likely to date someone just for the sake of it. It's not top on their list of priorities.

## Your Aquarius Child

I suppose the biggest complaint parents have about their Aquarius child is their refusal to take orders and their quirky way of looking at life. Other than that, there aren't many faults that surface with parenting an Aquarius.

Here's an 18-year-old young lady talking about herself: *"I'm an Aquarius. Independence is a big trait, I am rebellious when restricted, I have opinions, I'm smart, I'm shy, I'm sensitive, I have a big heart, I'm for lots of causes, I'm really passionate about my future career, I'm sweet, I care a lot about people, and I'm a family person."*

And here is the mother of a 5-year-old Aquarius child talking: *"My daughter is an Aquarius and she is very independent and loving. Since she could make a sound everything has been "I can do it by myself." She doesn't like anyone to help her and yet she is such a sweetheart, she's relaxed and smart and she doesn't like to play by herself, she has to be around people. She has a great personality."*

Here is someone else talking about their 9-year-old Aquarian daughter: *"She is bright, very inquisitive, ultra creative, and a friend to all."*

As I've said repeatedly and will say here again, everything depends on learning not only what sign and characteristics your child or relative is, but also what sign you are and understanding your own fears/hopes/aspirations. One of the useful things about learning Astrology, is you learn all about yourself, so having an understanding of your inner-self will stand you in good stead when you learn about your child.

If you're a Fire sign, your Aquarius child will fit happily into your family unit of wanting things to be exciting, action-based and alive.

If you're an Air sign parent, your little Aquarius child will seem a gem and they-can-do-no-wrong (most of the time). The problems can occur when you're a Water or Earth sign parent, and I will explain the differences.

If you are a Taurus, Virgo or Capricorn, your little bundle of Aquarius joy won't stay a bundle when they begin to grow-up and develop a voice.

If you're a Taurus you will want things to develop slowly and steadily, dinners on time, practical applications to everyday problems, and enough money to go round . That's not how Aquarians operate. They don't do things steadily, they are running about one day then comatose the next. They have weird and wonderful ideas that need discussion and validation. In the back of your mind will be worries about their level of truth....when it comes to ideas, truth doesn't come into it.

If you're a Virgo parent you will worry about their health, their friends, their health, their friends, and did I say worry? Yep you'll worry. That's what Virgos do. Aquarians don't (unless they've got Virgo Ascendant, planets or Sun in the 6$^{th}$)...so console yourself with the concept that your child will seem difficult and different from you.

If you're a Capricorn you might find your Aquarius child different but it generally won't upset you enough to change the way you are.

If you're a Cancer, you will do the nurturing thing but please don't expect your Aquarius child to be as emotional as you are. They can't. It's not in their nature.

If you're a Scorpio you might clash, but on some levels you have respect for each other, and if you're a Pisces... read my first book How To Survive a Pisces.

## Your Aquarius Boss

If your boss is a true Aquarian, and not a heavily disguised Capricorn or Pisces (people do confuse the three signs as their beginnings and endings are very near) they would generally allow you plenty of space, allow you to develop ideas, and leave you to your own devices. It's also highly unlikely that you'll have an Aquarius boss, well not in the standard sense, as a lot of

Aquarians are self-employed. In fact, because of their quirky nature, to be stuck in a nine-to-five position themselves won't fill them with glee. Maybe if they've got lots of planets in Capricorn, or Aries, you might find them working their way up the promotional ladder, but that's rare. In English History there have only been two Aquarians on the throne and interestingly, they were both women. Queen Mary 1st who had Moon in Aries, and Queen Anne who had Moon in Scorpio.

No, your Aquarius boss is a rare and peculiar being. If you find you've got one, expect your working life to one minute be in a rut, the next for it to suddenly change as your Aquarius boss gets inspired about something and wants you to join them in their 'exciting new idea'. I wonder sometimes if Aquarians work a lot in the computer industry but I don't have any facts to back that up. Suffice to say your Aquarian boss will give you the same things that he/she wants him/herself such as freedom of ideas, space to think, new ideas and friendship.

I know an Aquarian man who runs a café and over the years has had a number of staff in to help him. His family also helps, but he gets his ideas and inspiration from those employees as he works in his little kitchen. He likes to have fun and doesn't care where they come from as long as they can work hard. He's friendly to everyone he meets, likes to hear the latest ideas from them, but all the while doing what he wants to do, making the food he likes to make, doing his 'own thing' without trumpeting his achievements. He has spent his whole working life in a space no wider than 5 ft and no longer than 7 ft. That doesn't bother him as his day is filled with different customers, different staff (as eventually they leave and get 'proper' jobs, or marry or leave university and travel) and those important different ideas. They are his meat and veg, not the menu. He rides a bicycle to work. Even in this seemingly domestic set-up of food and family, he still maintains his Aquarian ideals of freedom and ideas. As a boss, his staff learn quickly what he does or doesn't like and he's interested in their lives and the lives of their families. He has a Scorpio Ascendant, so if he feels his privacy or freedom has been attacked, he's quick on the mark about getting retribution.

One Aquarius lady said she liked working in Universities as in those sorts of environments there are no bosses or underlings, everyone is working towards a similar concept: Knowledge. *"Universities are the nicest places I have worked. I like doing extra courses from time to time. I am interested in philosophy and have some philosophy qualifications along with my science one. I like interesting jobs that are not overly routine."*

So, to stay happy with your Aquarian boss, behave, act sensibly and wait for those quirky moments when things seem to have flipped into a parallel universe.

## Your Aquarius (female) lover

Well one thing is for certain, don't even think about removing their sense of freedom. A captured Aquarius is a little like a bird in a cage, beautiful to look at, but pining for the freedom they have lost.

Here is an Aquarius talking about the bonding process: *"I don't like the word bonding, it makes me feel a bit shackled and it almost feels forced."*

To date an Aquarius isn't difficult, provided you are interesting or interested they will want to be in your company. Aquarius is a fixed sign and doesn't like too much change. However to date a female Aquarius you do need to have:

a)    an opinion
b)    a viewpoint

The quickest way to turn-off an Aquarius is to be suffocating or jealous (unless they have a lot of Cancer or Scorpio in their chart). That just won't wash. You will also have to have some means of transport so you can visit places, a few bob to pay for tea and some enthusiasm for what you're doing. If you date an Aquarius, s/he won't be worried about how you look, or what you wear, leave that to the Librans and the Leos, s/he will want to know about your thinking process and are they similar to theirs. Do you think along the same lines? Is freedom part of your vocabulary? And are you doing something different or in a different way?

I can't remember where I read this so please excuse me if this is your idea, it certainly wasn't mine, that an Aquarius would enjoy a visit to an abattoir because it would be different. This isn't like Gemini who wants change for change's sake, they want different as in not-the-same-as-the-masses. Not mainstream. Not the same as everybody else.

If you want to date an Aquarius I suggest that you find out first what their main interests are. Also don't worry about who you are or what you do for a living. Those things are not important to an Aquarius. What is important is 'the ideal' that you will share and it must be something that you *can* share, the ideal that is, or the idea.

To get an understanding of what an Aquarius needs in a relationship I thought what better place to find the answer to that question than a dating site. As these people don't know I've been looking at their words and to ensure I'm not breaking any laws of copyright or license, I've only included the key parts of their profiles, the things they find most important when they are looking for a partner.

In the first part of this (long) profile, the lady in question describes her likes and what she does. She puts her age and physical description and that she likes the theatre, cinema, art and music and *"even a bit of dancing"*. She says she also enjoys a night in with *"good company, nice food and a good bottle of wine, a DVD and/or music and banter."*

Now, unless you were an Astrologer like me, you'd skim over

those words and think they would apply to most people. But the beginning of the description includes things this lady does on her own like the walking…she doesn't actually say she'd like to *share* those things with anyone and what you have to remember, make note of what people say and also what they don't say. Later on, she mentions the critical items that Mr Right (if he's out there) will need to pay close attention to if he wants this lady to be happy: *"I love all animals (especially my cat and two guinea pigs) and am very passionate about animal welfare."* This is someone who is passionate about 'animal welfare'. The Aquarian signature of supporting certain freedoms, in this case the freedom of animals to live happy lives. So, this would be a case of 'love me, love my pets'. You would have to love this lady's pets. Can you do that?

Having spent a number of paragraphs describing herself, she then describes her 'ideal man':*"Ideally, I am looking to meet my 'soulmate' to share this journey of life with, someone who is open and honest with themselves and others and who is generous of heart and spirit, caring, kind and considerate (or who is open and aware and working towards these things). I am also looking forward to chatting with like-minded people who share similar interests and beliefs, people who are open and friendly and maybe just want to chat about life and the Universe."*

She has mentioned more than once that she enjoys 'chatting', so conversation is important to her and notice how she slips from describing her ideal man….to looking forward to *'chatting with like-minded people'*. Make a big mental note. This lady is not looking for a one-to-one, deep, personal, intense, snuggly, passionate, uplifting, exciting man, so if you're Scorpio or Cancer or in fact any Water sign STAY AWAY! She wants to be part of the group, the group that has *'similar interests and beliefs'* the ideas and cerebral stuff is what she wants. She won't want you mooning around, heart-broken because you haven't seen her for a few days, worried that because she's out with her friends again and concerned that she hasn't returned your calls.

Now, in the next example this lady starts out with describing what she wants: "*I would love to meet my soul mate*" which doesn't actually say anything practical. Everyone wants to meet a soul-mate (unless they've read 'Hands Across Time, the Soul Mate Enigma' by Judy Hall 6.)

A little later on she uses Aquarian key-words like "*I'm also strong and independent, love a challenge and enjoy my own company.*"

Then she describes in more detail her ideal man: "*You should be successful with integrity and a degree of humility, motivated and positive with a sense of humour, respectful, trustworthy and non judgmental; a strong and confident man with well developed people skills; spiritual yet grounded, well educated and philosophical about life with the depth of character to cope with life challenges, and be gentle, passionate, and not afraid of commitment.*"

Phew, is any of that possible in one human being? Again this lady is clearly describing the qualities of what she thinks she wants but will probably never find, as it isn't based on fact, it's a good old Aquarian 'ideal'. She ends her piece with these clear Aquarian words: "*I am hoping initially to make contact with anyone who likes to talk and walk, go to cinema/theatre or any other bright ideas and if it just remains as friendship that is fine.*"

She's not even bothered if it remains as friendship **because friendship is what she really wants.**

Just in case you need further evidence of what an Aquarian woman wants or what they are like, here is another example. This lady starts her description and only two sentences in, she says: "*I am concerned about the environment and involved in social justice campaigns.*" A little further on another key phrase of what she wants them both to have in this relationship: "*being supportive to each other to enjoy their own individuality.*" In this example this lady keeps up with the true Aquarian theme: Individuality. I hasten to point-out, I have never met these people, they were on a dating website.

In the next example further evidence of how Aquarians see themselves: *"My brain works differently to most people's - I see an alternative angle, which doesn't always go down well but at least life is never boring."*

And finally this next lady made me wonder why she was actually on the dating website. It was as if she was more looking for a companion rather than a partner.

*"Love animals, had horses, dogs for years now, on my own with just one dog. Enjoy a challenge, like to travel but although I go alone, prefer to have company to share the experiences."*

She says she wants to 'share an experience'. No mention there of wanting to wash socks, or take kiddies to school, or wake at 5am to feed a baby or clean the bathroom, so these aren't ladies that are looking to start families. Equally no mention of enjoying cooking, so if you're a Taurus this wouldn't work either. A lot of their descriptions were about ideas and ideals. The saving of the planet, the like mindedness, the quirky ideas… they want to be part of a group, not a faithful, practical, emotional monogamy.

As I mentioned earlier I have two Aquarian sisters. My older sister had just started dating an Aquarian as I was writing this book and she wrote a poem about the beginning of that relationship.

## A Wet Summer. (Two Aquarians)

The road's a river past your door.
The garden's turned to mush.
The snails leave trails in the conservatory
and I have just squeezed one pint of water from my sock.

I thought it was breakfast but it's tea time.
There's been no sun for three days now.

The light is green like underwater;
the hills and fields are lost in wet.

Let's do nothing. But drink Sauvingnon blanc
and chuck damp logs on the smoking fire.
Or not get up but stay in bed and compare
toes, fingernails, noses. This isn't a holiday.
This is the summer washing down the drainpipe.

What's that weird yellow thing? It's the sun!
No, it's not. It just got blotted out by the next grey cloud
now dumping hailstones on the thatch.
And now the afternoon drips to night
and Oh! we're having sex again.

It's so dark I can't see the furniture or your face,
but I can feel you. I can feel you. Did I think
I could escape from myself?
Inside me is an ocean, indigo and deep.
Unexplored. Forgotten. Still.

I have strange dreams. My past loves all line up
and laugh at me. Your dead wife stands naked
in the garden in the moonlight. I can't hear
what she's saying. I think it is, "don't go there."

But I remember sun. Running in the sun
down a hot white sand beach.
Straight into the water. Straight into the waves.
And did you ever swim right out. Beyond the waves.
Beyond the stack and then turn round and look back
at the people like blobs of colour on the strand?
And as you basked in a curve of warmth
feel underneath you the heavy weight of cold dark water.

Indigo and deep.
Unexplored. Forgotten. Still. 7.

In my job I spend a lot of my time talking to people about relationships. To me, relationships are the life blood of humans. If we have happy relationships, everything else seems to fall into place, but if our close personal relationships are difficult, then life can be much harder. Some people just fall into relationships, just the same as they fall in love or even fall out of love. Having been in this job for so long I've now realised that two things are at play here. One, just the nature of humans and their interactions and two, the fashions of the time.

## Your Aquarius (male) lover

Now I'm going to give you some advice, some current advice about Aquarian males.

Just so you can understand the Aquarian concept from the viewpoint of both sexes, I've included here some examples from a dating website so you can understand the sort of qualities an Aquarian man looks for.

My first example made me smile when I read it, because it couldn't have been more Aquarian. He's being honest and he starts his piece with:*"I have no intention of misleading anyone so I will say upfront that I am on here to initially seek female friendship rather than a full on relationship."*

He carries on with what he would like in his partner, having said at the beginning that he doesn't want a 'full on relationship':*"So, if you're an easy going lady, with an open caring heart, happy to talk about what you want or desire, comfortable in your jeans and jumper and who may also like to get dressed up every now and then and can empathise with any of what's written here, then I think we would get on. You'll have to read the rest of this first however, because even in friendship you'll need to know something about me. I live by myself in a small village. I am active but not sporty and if you need a dancing, sailing, rock-climbing or golfing partner then I'm sorry but I'm not your man. I do enjoy photography, coastal and country walking and cooking. I have always been fairly domesticated and do enjoy my own space yet I do appreciate female company for a walk, sitting by candlelight, by the fire or outdoors in summer having a good chat and a glass of wine, or even a hug! (sorry, I had to say that, I really love hugging!)"*

This particular man is being completely honest with what he wants. He wants someone to accompany him on walks, chat to, hug a bit....and that's it. How different is that from what the ladies in the previous section were saying? It's not any different. It's completely the same. It is ideas based....

In the next example, the gentleman describes his height and where he's located, then: *"I enjoy looking after my garden (not too tidy!), history, watching films, cycling and yoga. I have travelled quite widely, but should we keep doing it? I am very interested in food for good health, the food programme on Radio 4 is my favourite. I like my own space but have more than enough at the moment and would like to meet someone who has similar interests to share."*

In the last example again the Aquarian concerns and themes are so part of this man's life, he's almost the epitome of the sign. Just one short description of what he wants:

*"I come with little packaging - my soul-mate and fellow traveller will like truth, openness and quiet intimacy."*

Then he launches into his qualities and what makes him tick. Pay attention here to the words I have highlighted as they represent the key elements that Aquarian men want:

*"I strive to be self- and other-aware. Vegan, cyclist, wood stove, into simplicity and abundant good food. Have **worked on energy/climate** for 25 years, initially a researcher/analyst, now mostly running courses and writing. I'm about to move **to live in a community**.*

*I'm pretty complicated which gives me a fair bit of sensitivity, interest and empathy for others' complexities.* **Heaven** *for me* **is** *long, slow, intimate* **conversations** *with lots of careful listening and no assumptions or jumping to conclusions - the sense of really getting to know someone, being known, and exploring* **experiences and ideas**.

*My work involves supporting a national network of* **groups** *exploring* **sustainable living**, *running workshops and courses aiming to empower people to respond to climate change, and writing.*

*Being on a personal and shared spiritual path is very important for me. My understanding of what that's about comes partly from Buddhism and Taoism but my primary commitment is as a Quaker. I'm very involved in my local* **meeting** *and have a daily practice. For me one of the most magic things about Quaker meeting is the sense that we can develop of a kind of* **collective consciousness** *- this connects for me to sustainability and the need to develop a* **collective will**. *I'm fascinated by psychology, myth, spirituality, culture and tend to read serious books very slowly.*

*My best kind of holiday is a* **quiet retreat** *with lots of* **walking** *and good food. I travel abroad sometimes but don't fly."*

This man is not looking for a person, he's looking for ideas. He wants his personal ideas about sustainability confirmed, his religious beliefs acknowledged and his desire to connect to the 'collective consciousness' matched by someone. He's not bothered about his partner's hair colour, or shape or country of origin. They have to have matching ideas. I mentioned at the beginning of this book how Aquarians want to be individual, but also want to be connected and it's a hard act to pull off success-fully. And again he wants the person who will have the *same ideas as him* because ideas are what *motivate* him.

One of my Gemini clients got frustrated about this very thing and said: *"I can remember saying disgustedly to my partner (Aquarius Sun combust Aquarius Moon, conjunct Aquarius Mercury, and together with Aquarius Venus all in Twelfth house), 'You'd sooner have a theory than the truth'!!"*

## What to do when your Aquarius relationship has ended?

As Aquarius is such a cerebral sign, the ending of a relationship can be deeply upsetting if you're a Water or Earth sign. If you're an Air or Fire sign it can be frustrating, anger-making and explosive.

I shall divide this section into the four Elements because that will allow you to ponder on the tactic that will suit you the best.

If you're a Fire sign: Aries, Leo or Sagittarius and you are now suffering the after-effects of an Aquarius relationship, my best advice is to do the following.

Get a candle, any type will do but the best would be a small nightlight and light it and recite:

"I......(your name) let you......(Aquarius name) go, in freedom and with love so that I am free to attract my true soul-love."

Leave the candle in a safe place to burn down, at least an hour's worth of burn time is good. Be careful not to leave the house and keep an eye on it.

Then over the next few days, gather-up any belongings that are your (now) ex's and either leave them round your (ex) Aquarius' house, or give them to charity.

If you have any photos, don't be in a big rush to tear them all up, as some Fire signs are prone to, then years later, when they feel better about the situation, regret not having any reminders of the (maybe few) nice times you had. When you have the strength, keep a few of the nicer photos, and discard the rest.

If you are an Earth sign: Taurus, Virgo or Capricorn you will feel less inclined to do something drastic or outrageous (unless of course you have a Fire sign Moon...)

The end of your relationship should involve the Element of Earth and this is best tackled using some crystals.

The best ones to use are the ones associated with your Sun

sign and also with protection. The following crystals are considered protective but are also birth stones. [8]

Taurus = Emerald

Virgo = Agate

Capricorn = Onyx

Take your Crystal and cleanse it in fresh running water. Wrap it in some tissue paper then take youself on a walk into the country. When you find a suitable spot, dig a small hole and place the crystal in the ground. Think about how your relationship has ended. Remember the good times and the bad. Forgive yourself for any mistakes you think you may have made. Imagine a beautiful plant growing where you have buried the crystal and the plant blossoming and growing strong. This is your new love that will be with you when the time is right.

If you are an Air sign: Gemini, Libra or Aquarius you might want to talk about what happened first before you succomb to end of play. Air signs need reasons and answers and can waste precious life-energy looking for answers.

Forgive yourself first of all for the relationship ending. It's no-one's fault and time will heal the wounds. When you are having a better day and your thoughts are clear, get a piece of paper and write your (ex) Aquarius a letter. This isn't a letter you are acually going to post, so you can be as honest as you want with your thoughts.

Write to them thus:

"Dear Aquarius,

I know you will be happy now that you're in your new life but there are a few things I want you to know and understand that you ignored when we were together."

Then list the annoying habits, ideas, dreams, fantasies that your (ex) Aquarius indulged in. Top of the list may be their inability to truly understand your needs, or maybe their 'coldness' or lack of empathy.

Make sure you write every little detail, down to the toothbrushes in the bathroom and the amount of times they said things like 'let's live in France!' or 'Why don't we buy a yurt?'

Keep writing until you can write no more, then end your letter with something similar to the following:

"Even though we went through hell together and never saw eye to eye, I wish you well on your path" or some other positive comment.

Then take the letter somewhere windy, high, out of town maybe where you won't be disturbed. The top of a hill overlooking a beautiful view, on a pier during a blustery day maybe, on a cliff face, but do be sensible and don't put yourself in any personal danger.

Read through your letter again. Make sure it sounds right in your head then ceremoniously tear a small part of your letter into the smallest pieces possible and let those small pieces of paper be whisked away by the wind. I don't think it's a good idea to dispose all of your letter in this way, because a) it might be rather long and you'd be guilty of littering and b) you also run the risk of it blowing somewhere inconvenient, so save the rest of it.

When you get home, burn the rest of the letter safely in an ashtray or put it in the paper shredder and add it to your paper recycling.

If you are a Water sign: Cancer, Scorpio or Pisces things will be a little harder for you to recover from. You might lie awake at night wondering if you've done the right thing by finishing the relationship, or feeling deeply hurt that the relationship has ended. Don't fret. Things will get better but you need to be able to get through those first difficult weeks without bursting into tears all the time.

Your emotional healing needs to encompass the water element. So here are a few suggestions.

This is a powerful way to heal the emotional hurt that has resulted in this relationship ending. It allows you to use that part of you that is most 'in tune' with the issue.

It involves your tears. The next time you feel weepy, collect your tears into a glass. This isn't as hard as it sounds. There you are, tears falling at a rapid rate, threatening to flood the world, all you need is one of those tears to fall into a glass of water. I recommend using a nice glass, something pretty, that has some meaning to you. Ensure the tear has fallen in, then top-up with enough water almost to the rim of the glass. Place the glass on a table, maybe with a lit candle, maybe with a photo of you together, whatever feels right for you, then recite the following.

This loving relationship with you:............has ended.
I reach out across time and space to you,
My tears will wash away the hurt I feel
And release you from my heart, mind and soul
We part in peace.
Then slowly drink the water.

Spend the next few weeks talking about how you feel to someone who cares. If there isn't anyone who can fill the role, consider a counsellor or therapist. Emotional Freedom Technique = E.F.T on the website www.emofree.com is very useful in these situations and you'll find it is an easy technique you can learn at home.

## Your Aquarius friend

If God were to invent the ideal friend, then he would have had in mind someone who is an Aquarius. Aquarius lives and breathes friendship. They are wacky, they can be spontaneous, they love a discussion, to look at and experience new things, new places. They will happily accompany you to the ends of the earth provided you just let them 'be'. Once you start to give them advice, or make suggestions, or criticise them about their weird and wonderful hobbies/choice of clothes/friends/house....they'll just drop you.

If you have some common interest, you're onto a winner. They can find everyone and everything interesting. The question is, for how long?

They do need their space, so don't crowd them out. They also will have their opinions(all Air signs do), so listen to them. They don't really like arguments (leave that to Librans) or if things are too changeable (leave that to Geminis) but they do love a good discussion, or debate.

Here is a (female) Gemini talking about her (female) Aquarius friend:

*"She is always so positive, always with a smile. She's the one who can always say something to make me laugh even if I am very depressed, and she never does it on purpose, it just comes naturally. The common things I noticed in the Aquarians I know, is they all are always joyful, making everyone around them smile also, and a bit "crazy" (in a good sense)."*

Now here have the weird friend's input. Another female Gemini talking about her daughter:

*"Aquarians seems to love having weird friends. When my daughter (Sun and Venus in Aquarius, but not conjunct) was about 11-13 'weird' was her favourite word. Both of these (not biologically related) individuals seemed to attract/be attracted to unusual, or even pretty off the wall people, or even crazy people."*

I sometimes think that without Aquarian weirdness, the world would be a very boring place. Who but an Aquarius could have thought of, let alone written a poem called the Jabberwocky?
'Twas brillig, and the slithy toves
Did gyre and gimble in the wabe;
All mimsy were the borogoves,
And the mome raths outgrabe.

Charles Lutwidge Dodgson aka Lewis Carroll a wonderfully talented, strange, original writer, had a Sagittarius Ascendant (optimistic, positive, confident) Sun in the 3rd house (good at communicating) and Moon in Sagittarius (adventurous emotional explorer of exciting things even if it means he might ruffle a few feathers)

This was something that was originally written for a magazine he produced for his immediate family and morphed into something now used in schools to demonstrate the rhythm and metre in poetry, even if using made-up words.

Here we have a female Pisces talking about her Aquarius friends:
*"I love them, .they are quirky! I gave my Aquarian best friend a pair of mismatching socks for her birthday! For me, they have a charisma."*

This female Virgo talked about Aquarians she has worked with. She didn't find them easy to understand:*"Although I have to admit this is coming from the sign of Virgo, so in that respect it is just my own Virgoan feelings and thoughts on the Aquarian people that I've encountered in my life! It is one of the signs that really intrigues me and never fully understood, yet I've never had anyone in my family or a close friend who is Aquarius. I think there is a good reason for this, especially as I've found the Aquarians I've met to be very difficult to really get to 'know'. I can't really speak about the men as it's been mostly Aquarian women that I've come across but here is how I perceive them to be in general:*

*The first thing that springs to mind is 'unusual'. I've found them to be highly intelligent but with a different take on life from most people. They see the things that others overlook, the small things. They are not scared to start an argument with anyone especially if they feel they have a point to prove. They can be extremely compassionate on the one hand but then turn round and be devastatingly cruel on another and can belittle or shock people when it suits. However they know when they have gone too far and will try to make amends in their own way. Their sense of humour can be a little warped but they do like to have fun and a good time whenever possible and for the most part are usually good company. They have love in their heart for people and the world as a whole but are not so good with the people around them on a one to one basis.*

*This even extends to children - they have no problem showing love to other peoples' children but are not so demonstrative with their own and I feel that some prefer to be childless and free from anything that ties and binds them - they remind me of Sagittarius in that respect.*

*There is a tendency to drugs/alcohol to escape from problems. They never talk about their feelings or problems and when they do it is in a very abstract way, like they don't own them. They have an amazing knack with computers/machinery and have patience when showing others how to do things. They tend to be hard working and take pride in what they do usually catching the manager's attention and easily gaining pay rises/promotions. They have many friends and are usually popular but even then they still keep their distance somehow. One aspect that really stands out is their honesty. They don't seem to have the capacity for slyness as it's just not in them. This shows when they are standing up for what they believe in and will always stand up for the underdog, even to their own cost, and that is probably their finest quality.*

*To sum up - when they are good they are great but when they are bad, well.......!*

As you can see from this summary, the earth sign Virgo has a hard time understanding the Aquarians she works with. She uses the words 'abstract' and 'distance', which are words a Virgo will struggle with as they like definition and detail and being able to categorise things and people. And I'm afraid you can't categorise an Aquarius. And here we have the criticism about not being demonstrative which is very important to an earth sign, especially tactile contact.

Do Aquarians have feelings? Here is an Aquarius discussing that point:

*"I dislike when people accuse Aquarians of not being emotional - I often feel emotive and I am reasonably good at empathising. Everyone has several planets - I have, for instance Venus in Pisces and Cancer Ascendant."*

To my mind, if an Aquarius has a few planets in water signs, then they will be capable of emotions, but without them, they are so cerebral they're almost like Mr Spock from Star Trek. They hear what you say, they understand what you're saying, they smile politely, and get on with their lives.

## Your Aquarius Mum

Now, if you are a Water sign (Cancer, Scorpio or Pisces) having an Aquarius Mum might be a bit hard.

Here is a female Scorpio talking about her Aquarius Mother:

*"My mom is Aquarius. I am a Scorpio. Three out of four of us kids have our Moon in Aquarius. My oldest brother raised us, my mom and dad divorced when we were young. I've only met my dad once, and my mom was physically and emotionally unavailable. She now lives a lonely and isolated life, but she was sexually abused so some of this is due to that abuse. We talk but are not close."*

It's not that they are difficult people. They're not. But they don't understand emotions like the water signs do. They'll love your ideas, your suggestions, what you're doing, who you're friends with/married to/dating/hanging-around-with but that's as far as it goes. They won't weep with you when your pet dies, they won't wipe away your tears gently when you're watching a sad movie, and they certainly won't understand you feeling sad, or moody or upset. So, how will a water sign manage with an Aquarius mother?

I suppose the best way to cope is to have some good friends you can confide in and get your emotional strokes from them. If your Mum has a few water planets, then you're in luck, even more so if their Moon is in a watery sign. If they are all Air, just accept they will come across (to you) as detached, emotionless, unfeeling and other words when in fact it's a bit like asking an elephant to fly. It's never going to happen. Ah, I hear you say (because you are a sensitive water sign). Dumbo was an elephant, and he had big ears and he could fly…. Let's be realistic here, so to bond with an Aquarius Mum, fantasy won't wash. In fact Aquarian's older ruler was Saturn, the planet of responsibility and doing-things-the-hard-way. So there is that aspect to an Aquarius. Anyway I'm supposed to be telling you how to cope with an Aquarius mother…

Move out early. Leave home. They want you to have your independence, so leaving home won't upset them (it would upset a Cancer Mum). In fact your relationship will be a whole lot better, so club together with some friends, or get your own room to rent and move out as soon as you can.

If you're an Earth sign, again things will be tricky. Here's a Capricorn female talking about her Aquarius mother:

*"I am a Caricorn daughter of an Aquarius mother and Aries father. My mother dominated the household but neither parent did much parenting. My father always worked late so he wasn't around for after school events. My mother was but she never took any interest. I remember once when I was to MC a school program we almost didn't make it to the school on time and she gave no particular value to my part in the function.*

*I have an Aquarius aunt and uncle as well (her siblings). All are very set in their opinions and will not tolerate other points of view. Opinions were always more important than feelings. Both of them have never married. One is a priest and the other a 70 year old who is virtually friendless. It is interesting that the three of them tend to cling to each other even through they don't normally get along."*

Here is another Capricorn whose mother just couldn't parent her the way she wanted:

*"She seemed to be very detached from me on an emotional level."*

Now what does that actually mean? To be detached on an emotional level? Feelings can be very subtle and I think it's those subtle differences that Aquarians struggle with. They're OK with 'happy' or 'sad', and even 'cross' or 'contented' but when you get to 'jealous' or 'possessive' or worse 'sentimental' or 'passionate' they won't know what you're talking about and if you're an Earth or Water sign, they won't care as much as you do.

Aquarians are almost as bad as Pisces Mums for not-being-on-the-planet but unlike the Pisces Mum who is in 'fairy-land', the Aquarius Mum is in 'ideas land'. This is a place where all Aquarians' minds live, where they cogitate and ruminate, reflect and deliberate and generally wander around in their minds planning, thinking, processing, coming-up-with-great-opinions and lengthy outlines of whatever has sparked them that day.

Here's the Capricorn lady talking again: *"She has always been involved in clubs and organizations and there was no question about whose agenda had top priority. While she was indifferent to most of our daily affairs, she has many phobias and would suddenly get over involved in our activities when they pushed one of her buttons."*

I asked this Capricorn lady what she would have wanted from her Mom: *"..(when I was a child) if I was looking for her opinion for how my piano piece sounded, or how I looked in an outfit, or if I would ask her to join me to go to a function, it seems she could never get excited about anything. If I was upset about something that may have happened at school, she would never comfort me. She would be very interested and concerned as to what had happened to me and would want to know where, when, how, etc. She would always analyze and give an explanation as to why something may have happened, but she would never soothe me with kind words."*

And don't expect your Aquarius Mum to know how you are feeling. She can't. Only you know how you feel. This lady wanted soothing with kind words but her Aquarius Mum wanted to know about her ideas, not her feelings. That difference is where problems begin.

If you are a Taurus eating is very important. Eating, sleeping, touch, skin, food, taste, smell, cooking, holding, being in physical contact with you or your things are life itself. Aquarians and all the Air signs, when they are onto an idea, can forego food, drink and any form of sustenance for a considerable amount of time. So, if you're a Taurus and your Mum is Aquarius, a gentle reminder that you need breakfast/ lunch/dinner will be a necessity. You might even have to go as far as putting up notices in the kitchen about meal-times or if you're really resourceful, learn to cook early and make your own food.

If you're a Fire sign or an Air sign, don't worry, your Aquarius mother will seem like a goddess to you. Here is a Leo man who works in design talking about his Aquarius mother's parenting skills:

*"I didn't breast feed too well. Apart from that she's a lusher!"*

She will love your excitement, your enthusiasm, the thrill-of-the-chase and will support every project or idea you come up with. As eating and practical things aren't what turns you on, there will be no conflict and life will be easier.

Here is an Aquarius Mum talking about her Gemini son:*"I am an Aquarian mother married to an Aquarian man - we share a birthday. We have one child, a Gemini son. I am very freedom loving and freedom granting. I am an open minded parent that believes strongly in education, spirituality and a loving spirit. My son is bright and kind* and full of wisdom and stops me in my tracks with his words. Besides his Sun in Gemini, he has Ascendant and Moon in Sagittarius. The three of us get along great, and, at times, it feels like a party in our home."

## Your Aquarius Dad

I know a few Aquarian Dads. Again they're not marvellous at the practical side of life, unless they have Earth sign planets or Ascendant, but they seem to know the difference between emotion and intellect. Not that they'll always *use* emotion but they do know it exists.

Here is a very self-reflective Aquarius Dad talking about his boys: "The biggest challenge of parenting for me is to not come on too strong and alienate my children as my father often did with me. I want them to have a kinder / gentler father than I had. It is hard to find the right middle ground between being too stern or too lax. I must admit that even though I want my kids to have the freedom to choose for themselves, it was kind of a kick in the head when my 18 year old told me he was considering moving out on his own. I tried to discourage him from that as I was concerned that he would forsake college. After I realized that he was determined to take this course, I was able to help him find an affordable apartment where he is now free to live without many constraints. Yes, I want him to be his own man, but now that he is, and doesn't seem to need me so much, I sometimes feel sorry for myself as if I have lost something. I even found myself projecting untoward qualities onto him because of this which is, of course, completely unacceptable. He helped me fix my car this weekend and I told him again how proud I am of him. With my youngest boy, it is very enjoyable when he comes to me asking to teach him certain "manly" things like how to use the lawnmower. I see him desiring to mature and be more grown up, and I try to encourage this development, without placing too much pressure on him, as that will come soon enough.

*I do not think that I am "father of the year" material, but hopefully I am a "good enough" dad."*

Two notable male music stars are Aquarius: Phil Collins and Robbie Williams and they both have Moon in Scorpio and they both are having trouble 'settling down'. Phil has a number of children by various wives and, as yet, Robbie has no wife or children. It's hard to find an example of an Aquarius Dad because the words 'cosy' and 'cuddly' don't come to mind when you're talking about Aquarians. So, if your Dad is Aquarius, again think about what element you are (Earth, Air, Fire, Water) and adapt yourself to their thinking...

One thing is for sure, Aquarian Dads like anything that is different, computerized, pluggable-inable and electric. Don't forget Aquarius is now 'ruled' by Uranus and Uranus governs computers, electricity, and things that happen suddenly and without warning.

If you want to stay on the right side of your Aquarius Dad, make sure you lend them your iPod, Mac-Book Air and anything digital, they will love you forever!

On a serious note, you will find difficulties if you're a water sign, (see Aquarius Mum above) but all is not lost if you remember they're just not going to be as emotional as you.

## Your Aquarius sibling

If your brother or sister is an Aquarius, don't panic. I've not come across too many people that complain about their Aquarian siblings. However, as always, take into account what star sign you are.

The Fire and Air signs get on better with Aquarius energy. They blend and mix well. The trickiness appears when you're an Earth or Water sign.

Let's go back to the forums and find out who gets on with who and what sort of problems occur.

Here is a Pisces girl talking about her Aquarius sister:

*"I very much believe that Aquarians have feelings, but they are very reserved about showing them. My crazy Aquarius sister can make the most terrible remarks about people and laugh, but I just think "Wow you're so mean you should be slapped" and laugh a little. I really think a lot of Aquarians don't feel good about displaying emotion. They have emotions like everyone else."*

She admits that Aquarians 'have emotions like everyone else' but the 'not displaying' them was the issue. So, if your brother or sister is an Aquarius don't expect them to display their emotions the same way you do. You also have to consider what you think a 'good' relationship is for someone, or for you even.

There are millions of different preferences for people. Some like to have their own space. Virginia Woolf talked about this in great detail in 'A Room of One's Own'. She reckoned you couldn't write unless you had your own room....and an income...Hmm, then when I checked the charts of the people she references such as Emily Bronte, well she was a Leo and Jane Austen was a Sagittarius, both strong Fire signs and less likely to let others stand in their way.

If we look at family dynamics, Aquarius energy does best when the sibling is grown as the childish Aquarius energy is concerned with that which is interesting, not that which is touching, or childish.

Let's go back to the Aquarian key-words: sociable, commu-nicative, altruistic, progressive, independent, rational, detached, eccentric, dogmatic, erratic and cranky.

When you read those words, does the word 'child' spring to mind? No, I didn't think it did.

So, to get on with your Aquarian brother or sister here are my easy to use tips:

Don't tell them what to do...

Don't tell them what to think...

Don't steal their friends (this is an almost unforgivable sin in their eyes)

Do be interested in what they're doing, thinking, planning

Do be honest about how you feel about things.

Do keep the lines of communication open, but don't crowd them out, they do need their space.

I hope you have enjoyed learning a little about Astrology and a little about Aquarius the star sign.

A final quote I'd like to share from an Aquarian lady I spoke to: *"I hope I am staying roughly on the same course in life - useful, interested, involved but not too-involved, but we none of us ever can tell."*

I hope this helps you understand the penultimate sign of the Zodiac a bit more. If you need more information , please visit my website www.maryenglish.com

I am writing this, while the Moon is in Aquarius, in my office in the city of Bath, the hot spring city in South West England. I am a Pisces. I am happy in my job, with my son, with my lovely husband and with my family. I know that all life is made from good and bad and I decided, not so long ago, to focus on the good. There is a candle burning by me and I am imagining that the flame is burning to help you focus on the good too. If we all understood each other a little more, maybe we'd get on better. I wish you all the peace in the world.......and happiness too.

# References

1. A Room of One's Own by Virginia Woolf, published 2008, Oxford University Press, Oxford OX2 6DP

2. The Dawn of Astrology, by Nicholas Campion, A cultural history of western astrology, published 2008, Hambledon Continuum, London SE1 7NX

3. The Instant Astrologer, by Felix Lyle and Bryan Aspland, 1998, Judy Piatkus, London

4. The Gods of Change, Pain Crisis and the Transits of Uranus, Neptune and Pluto, by Howard Sasportas, Published 1989, Arkana, Penguin, London W8, England.

5. Soul Mates - Honouring the Mysteries of Love and Relationship, by Thomas Moore, published 1999, Harper Collins, New York USA

6. Hands Across Time - The Soul Mate Enigma, by Judy Hall, 1997, Findhorn Press, Forres, Scotland, www.judyhall.co.uk

7. Poem kindly donated by Lucy English www.lucyenglish .com

8. Cunningham's Encyclopedia of Crystal, Gem and Metal Magic, by Scott Cunningham, published 1998, Llewellyn Publications, USA

# Further Information

## Further Reading

Alive and Well with Uranus, by Bil Teirney, 1999, Llewellyn,St Paul, USA

The Modern Text Book of Astrology, by Margaret E Hone, 1980, LN Fowler Ltd, Romford, Essex, UK

Alive and Well with Uranus, Transits of Self Awareness, by Bil Tierney,1999, Llewellyn Publications, St. Paul, MN, USA.

An Astrological Study of the Bach Flower Remedies, by Peter Damian, 1997, published by Neville Spearman Publishers/CW Daniel Company Ltd, 1 Church Path, Saffron Walden, Essex CB10 1JP

Astrological Crosses in Relationships, by Pauline Edwards, 2002, Llewellyn Publications, PO Box 64383, St Paul, MN USA, www.llewellyn.com

Astrology for Dummies, 1999, IDG Books Worldwide, Inc, CA 94404

## Information and Resources

The Bach Centre, The Dr Edward Bach Centre, Mount Vernon, Bakers Lane, Brightwell-cum-Sotwell, Oxon, OX10 0PZ, UK www.bachcentre.com

Emotional Freedom Technique www.emofree.com

Ethical Dating Site www.natural-friends.com

Spiritual Community in North Scotland www.findhorn.org

William Herschel Museum of Astronomy in Bath

19 New King Street, Bath, BA1 2BL, England. Tel: 01225 446 865 www.williamherschel.org.uk

# Astrological Chart information

The Astrological Association
   www.astrologicalassociation.com
Birth chart data from astro-databank at
   www.astro.com and www.astrotheme.com
Robbie Williams 13-02-1974, Stoke-on-Trent, 3.10pm Leo
   Ascendant, Sun 7th, Moon Scorpio
Phil Collins 30-01-1951, Chiswick, London, 30-01-1951, Libra
   Ascendant, Sun 4th, Moon Scorpio
Marion D March, 10-02-1923, Nuremberg, Germany, 3.46am,
   Sagittarius Ascendant, Sun 3rd, Moon Sagittarius
Joan Mc Evers, 07-02-1925, Chicago IL, USA, 6.34am, Aquarius
   Ascendant, Sun 1st, Moon Leo
Oprah Winfrey, 29-01-1954, Kosciusko MS, USA, 4.30am,
   Sagittarius Ascendant, Sun 2nd, Moon Sagittarius
Paul Newman, 26-01-1925, Cleveland OH, USA, 6.30am,
   Capricorn Ascendant, Sun 1st, Moon Pisces
Paris Hilton, 17-02-1981, New York NY, USA, 2.30am, Sagittarius
   Ascendant, Sun 3rd, Moon Leo
James Joyce, 02-02-1882, Dublin, Ireland, 6.24am, Capricorn
   Ascendant, Sun 2nd, Moon Leo
Abraham Lincoln, 12-02-1809, 6.54am, Hodgenville KY, USA,
   Aquarius Ascendant, Sun 1st, Moon Capricorn
Charles Darwin, 12-02-1809, Shrewsbury, England, 03.00am,
   Sagittarius Ascendant, Sun 3rd, Moon Capricorn
Germaine Greer, 29-01-1939, Melbourne, Australia, 6.00am,
   Aquarius Ascendant, Sun 12th, Moon Taurus
Jacqueline du Pre, 26-01-1945, Oxford, England, 11.30am, Aries
   Ascendant, Sun 10th, Moon Cancer
Mia Farrow, 9-02-1945, Los Angeles, California, USA, Moon
   Taurus,
Virginia Woolf, 25-01-19982, London, England, 12.15pm, Gemini
   Ascendant, Sun 8th, Moon Aries

Placido Domingo, 21-01-1941, Madrid, Spain, 10pm, Virgo Ascendant, Sun 5$^{th}$, Moon Scorpio

Mike Farrell, 06-02-1939, St.Paul MN, USA, 8.40am, Pisces Ascendant, Sun 12$^{th}$, Moon Virgo

W. Somerset Maugham, 25-01-1874, Paris, France, no accurate birth-time, Moon Taurus

Charlotte Rampling, 05-02-1946, Haverhill, England, no accurate birth-time Moon Pisces

Yoko Ono, 18-02-1933, Tokyo, Japan, 8.30pm, Libra Ascendant, Sun in 5$^{th}$, Moon in Sagittarius

Jack Nicklaus, 21-01-1940, Columbus, OH, USA, 3.10am, Scorpio Ascendant, Sun 3$^{rd}$, Moon in Gemini

Vanessa Redgrave, 30-01-1937, Blackheath, UK, 6pm, Leo Ascendant, Sun 6$^{th}$, Moon in Virgo

Roberta Flack, 10-02-1937, Black Mountain NC, USA, 6.30am, Ascendant Aquarius, Sun 1$^{st}$, Moon in Aquarius

Nolan Ryan, 31-01-1947, Refugio TX, USA, 9.45am, Pisces Ascendant, Sun 11$^{th}$, Moon in Gemini

Jean English (my Mother) 16-02-1921, Shrewsbury, UK, 11am, Gemini Ascendant, Sun 9$^{th}$, Moon in Gemini

Barbara Gibbings (my Auntie) 27-01-1917, Hampshire, 2am, Scorpio Ascendant, Sun 3$^{rd}$, Moon Pisces

Client's location of birth withheld due to confidentiality

Client A, female,29-01-1965, UK, 12.30am, UK, Scorpio Ascendant, Sun 4$^{th}$, Moon in Sagittarius

Client B, female, 23-01-1959, 12.30am, UK, Libra Ascendant, Sun 4$^{th}$, Moon in Cancer

Client C, female, 25-01-1964, 3.55pm, UK, Cancer Ascendant, Sun 7$^{th}$, Moon in Gemini

Client D, female, 07-02-1959, 9.35pm, UK, Libra Ascendant, Sun 5$^{th}$, Moon in Aquarius

Client E, female, 24-01-1973, 3am, UK, Scorpio Ascendant, Sun 3$^{rd}$, Moon in Libra

Client F, male, 16-02-1970, 9.05pm, UK, Virgo Ascendant, Sun 6$^{th}$,

Moon in Cancer

Client G, female, 10-02-1977, 6am, UK, Capricorn Ascendant, Sun 2nd, Moon in Scorpio

# Index

# BOOKS

O is a symbol of the world, of oneness and unity. In different cultures it also means the "eye," symbolizing knowledge and insight. We aim to publish books that are accessible, constructive and that challenge accepted opinion, both that of academia and the "moral majority."

Our books are available in all good English language bookstores worldwide. If you don't see the book on the shelves ask the bookstore to order it for you, quoting the ISBN number and title. Alternatively you can order online (all major online retail sites carry our titles) or contact the distributor in the relevant country, listed on the copyright page.

See our website www.o-books.net for a full list of over 500 titles, growing by 100 a year.

And tune in to myspiritradio.com for our book review radio show, hosted by June-Elleni Laine, where you can listen to the authors discussing their books.